Multicultural
Plays
for Children

VOLUME I: GRADES K–3

Smith and Kraus *Books For Actors*
YOUNG ACTORS SERIES

Great Scenes and Monologues for Children
Great Scenes for Young Actors from the Stage
Great Monologues for Young Actors
Multicultural Monologues for Young Actors
Multicultural Scenes for Young Actors
Monologues from Classic Plays 468 BC to 1960 AD
Scenes from Classic Plays 468 BC to 1970 AD
New Plays from A.C.T.'s Young Conservatory Vol. I
New Plays from A.C.T.'s Young Conservatory Vol. II
Plays of America from American Folklore for Young Actors 7-12
Seattle Children's Theatre: Six Plays for Young Actors
Short Plays for Young Actors
Villeggiatura: A Trilogy by Carlo Goldoni, *condensed for Young Actors*
Loving to Audition: The Audition Workbook for Young Actors
Movement Stories for Children
An Index of Plays for Young Actors
Discovering Shakespeare: A Midsummer Night's Dream;
   a workbook for students
Discovering Shakespeare: Romeo and Juliet; *a workbook*
   for students
Discovering Shakespeare: The Taming of the Shrew;
   a workbook for students

CAREER DEVELOPMENT SERIES

The Job Book: 100 Acting Jobs for Actors
The Job Book II: 100 Day Jobs for Actors
The Smith and Kraus Monologue Index
The Great Acting Teachers and Their Methods
The Actor's Guide to Qualified Acting Coaches: New York
The Actor's Guide to Qualified Acting Coaches: Los Angeles
The Camera Smart Actor
The Sanford Meisner Approach
Cold Readings: Some Do's and Don'ts for Actors at Auditions

If you require prepublication information about upcoming Smith and Kraus books, you may receive our semi-annual catalogue, free of charge, by sending your name and address to *Smith and Kraus Catalogue, P.O. Box 127, One Main Street, Lyme, NH 03768. Or call us at (800) 895-4331, fax (603) 795-4427.*

Multicultural Plays for Children

for Children

VOLUME I: GRADES K–3

by Pamela Gerke

Young Actors Series

SK

A Smith and Kraus Book

A Smith and Kraus Book
Published by Smith and Kraus, Inc.
One Main Street, PO Box 127, Lyme, NH 03768

Copyright ©1996 by Pamela Gerke All rights reserved
Manufactured in the United States of America
Cover and Text Design by Julia Hill
Cover Art by IreneKelly
First Edition: March 1996
10 9 8 7 6 5 4 3 2

Library of Congress Cataloging-In-Publication Data
Gerke, Pamela.
Multicultural plays for young actors / by Pamela Gerke.
p. cm. -- (Young actors series)
Includes bibliographical references.
Contents: v. 1. Grade levels K–3.
Summary: Ten plays based on multicultural folktales from such
countries as Ghana, China, and Italy.
ISBN 1-57525-005-5 (v.1)
1. Pluralism (Social sciences--Juvenile drama.) 2. Ethnic groups--Juvenile drama.
3. Children's plays, American. 4. Drama in education.
[1. Folklore-Drama. 2. Plays.] I. Title. II. Series.
PS3557.E674M85   1996
812'.54--dc20   96-164
CIP
AC

Acknowledgements

Thanks to all the people who helped me with foreign language translations and pronunciations and cultural information: Stesha Brandon, Inga Furlong, Maria Gillman, Vi Hilbert, Stacia Keogh, Eileen Kilgren, Nancy Mar, David Miles, Vladimir Vladimirov, Rae Wu and Louise Zamporutti.

Thanks for computer support to: Phyllis Roberts, Allan Tamm, and Richard Weeks.

Thanks to all the kids who were involved in the original productions of these scripts.

Dedicated to Mud, Mary L. Gerke, with love.

Contents

WORKING WITH CHILDREN IN PLAY PRODUCTION *(Cont.)*

THE SCRIPTS

Introduction

This book is designed for use by classroom teachers and other adults who work with children and want to do plays with them. Each script comes with detailed suggestions for creating all the elements of production: sets, props, costumes, lights, and sound, as well as staging directions, vocabulary lists of foreign language words used in the scripts, and general information about how to alter and adapt each script for various circumstances (cast size, rehearsal time, number of girls or boys in the cast, and so forth). Included in the introductions to the plays are discussions on the subject of the significance of play production as a child development activity, including psychological, emotional, kinesthetic, social, and educational aspects. Also included in this book are general instructions and suggestions for working with children in play productions.

I began to write and direct children's plays several years ago when I was directing an after-school program at an elementary school. At the time it seemed to be one of the most fun things we could do—and it was! I then created a children's play production company, Kids Action Theater, where I've written, directed, and produced all of the plays in this book. Working with children in play production continues to be a source of artistic inspiration, pleasure, and income for me and the old adage still rings true: By working with children, I learn about myself.

I believe that as citizens of the twenty-first century it is imperative that we integrate the arts into our educational systems. Our Western culture and education have been biased toward so-called "left brain" thinking for far too long. If we are to truly fulfill our human potential, stop the destruction of our environment, and create a sustainable, peaceful community, we must develop whole-brain thinking skills. To do this, the arts and other creative, nonlinear, nondualistic ways of thinking and being must be given at least as much attention in our schools as the modes of thinking that are traditionally emphasized.

The Significance of Play Production in Child Development

HUMAN DEVELOPMENT AND THE MEANING OF FUN

I believe our human system is designed so as to make us want to do that which is good for our own development. This is particularly noticeable in children. We can learn about what is good nourishment for children's development by observing what it is that they *want* to do, what is fun for them. They want to swing on swings and spin on merry-go-rounds because such repetitive movements aid in neurological patterning and the development of the vestibular system and equilibrium. Children want to climb on jungle gyms because it's good for their gross motor and brain development to do so. They want to be watched and praised because it helps them develop a positive self-image.

Children, allowed to play freely, will most often choose to dramatize their fantasies—to playact. Children playact because it's fun, and I say it's fun because it's psychologically, emotionally, and kinesthetically good for them. Playacting allows children to experience being in complete control of their world, where they can successfully solve problems and creatively express their feelings and desires.

PSYCHOLOGICAL ASPECTS

Working with children in play production is good for their development. It allows them to be physically active and learn kinesthetically, i.e., through their bodies. Plays create safe situations where children can act out adventure, danger, combat, and even death. The experience of fantasy, imagery, symbolism, and movement speaks to the psyche, invoking primal instincts, playing out archetypal roles, and satisfying unconscious needs to resolve problems. Plays can creatively address what one of my teachers, Molly Scudder, calls the "tender topics": sex, violence and death, subjects which we in our Western society seem to avoid with children but which they are often greatly concerned with coming to terms with. Play productions give children the opportunity to take risks, act in ways that would otherwise not be "allowed" in real life, and express hidden feelings.

ATTENTION, SELF-ESTEEM & PERSONAL EMPOWERMENT

Producing plays with children helps them learn to focus their attention, one of the most important tasks of child development. As is true for adults, it's a lot easier to pay attention when what you are doing is enjoyable, and playacting is one of the most fun activities of all for children.

Play production is also a natural device for positive "mirroring," reflecting back to children support from which they can build a good self-image. As they take their bows, being watched and literally applauded for their good efforts, children beam with pleasure and receive a big, healthy boost to their self-esteem.

Play productions help develop what Mary Budd Rowe calls "fate control," that is, the belief that individuals have control over the events in their lives. In the realm of the arts there is really no "right and wrong" as established by an external authority (critics included!). Drama and other arts activities can help children realize their own, internal powers of imagination and personal truth and a sense of control over their lives if the adults working with them allow them to freely express their ideas and share ownership of the creation of the play production.

ARTS EDUCATION

All arts activities have the power to connect to the inner depths of the psyche through imagination, symbolism, and humor. The arts need to be recognized as equal to all other subjects in our educational system. Arts activities support learning styles and brain functions which are otherwise mostly neglected in our schools but that are vital to the development of creative thinking, a balanced personality, and a healthy psyche. The arts can be integrated with other subjects to promote whole-brain thinking. Literature, reading, social studies, history, foreign language, music, movement and art are some of the subjects covered by producing the plays in this book.

Collaborative arts activities, such as plays, help children to develop good social skills. Artistic collaboration calls for group decision making and cooperation in order to be successful. In addition, there's a certain sense of comradery that naturally develops among a cast that warms and strengthens their social interactions.

FOLK TALES & MULTICULTURAL EDUCATION

All the plays in this books are adaptations of folktales from various countries or cultures from around the world. These are stories that have been handed down through the ages, continually altered and adapted by succeeding generations while retaining core truths about human nature and existence. Folktales, fairytales, and myths are stories that have lasted because they speak of profound truths, teach us about life and ethics, and are vastly entertaining. With the proliferation of commercial entertainment in our modern, Western culture, we are losing an important psychological and social tool in the form of folktales and mythology.

Producing plays of folktales is a good way to study other groups of people, their culture, language, literature, traditions and wisdom. Teaching children these ancient stories helps in their moral and spiritual development, spreads cultural literacy, cross-cultural awareness and understanding, and promotes a high level of artistic quality.

Working with Children in Play Productions

DIRECTOR'S ATTITUDE

Besides all the serious and profound reasons for doing plays with kids, the most important thing is: It's just plain fun! And if the adults maintain a playful attitude, they will enjoy it as much as the kids.

I'll never forget when my attitude was first altered regarding this. I was directing a play with four- to six- year-olds and as we approached performance day, I became increasingly frustrated and angry with the cast for not living up to my demands for perfection. The day came when I lost my temper and threatened to cancel the performance. All of a sudden, in the middle of my tirade, little Oscar projectile vomited. Bright orange and pink vomit went spewing out of his mouth and all over the stage and in that moment I realized that nothing really mattered (except Oscar's well-being). Since then, whenever I'm directing a children's play and begin to feel angry, wanting the production to meet my (adult) standards of perfection, I remember Oscar and the bright orange and pink projectile vomit and my sense of perspective and priority is righted.

Directing plays with children can be a very satisfying and enjoyable experience. But if you, the director, are not clear about what your goals are and what you expect from your cast members, the play experience can become frustrating and nerve-wracking. Ideally, the purpose of doing plays with children should be to provide an enriching, educational, and fun experience and one that promotes self-esteem. You, too, will also learn from and enjoy this experience if you focus on these goals.

It's understandable if you, as director, become anxious and demanding in rehearsals due to your desire to have the production meet your standards of excellence and your sense of responsibility for it's outcome. The best thing you can do is to maintain a positive, relaxed attitude at all times and always be fully supportive of every member of your cast and crew. Keep the production in perspective:

Remember, it's not Broadway—it's a bunch of kids doing their best and hopefully having fun in the process.

At the same time, expect nothing but the best from your actors. Demand that they pay attention, cooperate with others and try their hardest. Maintain a rehearsal atmosphere that is disciplined and focused. Be confident in your role as leader and your cast will sense this and react accordingly, respecting your authority and the limits you set. Likewise, if you are unsure of yourself as director your cast will feel insecure and may behave badly.

One of the most difficult aspects of directing children in plays is that they sometimes have a hard time focusing on the activity, especially in the beginning. They'll be bouncing off the walls and talking more than listening, and this makes it difficult for the adults in charge. However, learning to concentrate attention is, to my mind, the most valuable reason for doing play productions with children. Their minds are not already focused on the play in the beginning of the process because focusing their attention is precisely what they have come to learn. The director should understand this and provide a supportive atmosphere for children to grow in their ability to pay attention.

Always solicit the actor's comments and suggestions for both the play and for the creation of it's production elements so that they have a sense of ownership of their play production. Encourage positive comments from the children about the work of other cast members but do not allow them to make negative comments about others because it can have a devastating effect on the other children's feelings and self-esteem.

HOW TO USE THESE SCRIPTS

These scripts are designed to be adaptable to many different situations. They can be done as an unrehearsed run-through which is not performed for an audience, wherein the teacher reads the narration and describes the action while the students act it out. These scripts can also be used as a reading activity, either unrehearsed or rehearsed for a staged reading with an audience. To do a staged reading, the actors sit in chairs facing the audience. One person reads all the stage directions as needed, and the actors read their parts and may do a minimal amount of movement, including the use of small props. Readings make interesting performances that require less preparation time than a staged production.

For fully staged productions you can alter the scripts as long as you maintain respect for the traditions from which the stories come. All the staging directions in the scripts and ideas for making sets, props, costumes, lights, sound, and music are only guidelines. Think of these ideas as simply source material from which you and your ensemble create your own, unique and creative production.

Because these scripts are all adapted from folklore of specific cultures, you can generate a lot of good ideas for your play by bringing in stories, maps, artifacts, guest speakers, current events, and other information about the culture of the play's origin and in this way use the script as the basis for an interdisciplinary social studies unit.

SCRIPT PROCEDURE

1. Make a photocopy of the entire script, including (when applicable) the foreign language vocabulary list in Appendix A.
2. After casting the play, make any changes necessary on your Master Script (see script changes below). You may want to write the names of the actors in the margin next to their characters' names. Make script changes using correction fluid or white stickers and a dark pencil or pen (black is best).
3. Make copies of your Master Script for your cast as needed. To save paper and copying cost, you can copy for each actor only the pages with their lines. If some of the actors have few or no lines to memorize, you can simply have them learn their lines by rote in rehearsal and not copy script pages for them.
4. Write the name of each cast member on their script copy and highlight their lines for them with a highlighter pen, or have them highlight their own.

SCRIPT CHANGES

1. To make a single character into a small group: Change all references to that character from singular to plural, including pronouns and (where applicable) foreign language words. The actors in the group can either say their lines in unison, or lines can be assigned to individuals (specify in the script).

2. To change a small group role into a single character: Change all references to that character from plural to singular, including pronouns and (where applicable) foreign language words. Assign all of those group lines (such as Villager #1, Villager #2, etc.) to one actor.
3. To change the gender of a character: Change all gender references to that character including pronouns and (where applicable) foreign language words.
4. To make the play shorter in length: Eliminate lines, and/or parts of scenes. The Narrator can summarize the portions that have been cut in order to retain the story line. Songs and/or dances can be eliminated.
5. To make the play longer in length: Add lines, parts of scenes, and/or scenes. New roles or scenes can be written or improvised by the actors. Songs and/or dances can be added.
6. To set the play in another country: Change all references to the location of the story, possibly including foreign language words.
7. To change the foreign language words to English, refer to the vocabulary list in Appendix A.

MEMORIZATION

I have found the best procedure for memorizing lines is to send the actors' script pages home with them, with a note to their parents/guardians asking them to help with the memorization of lines. I ask that they spend a few minutes each day with their child, going over their lines by giving them their cues, i.e., the lines that proceed the actor's lines. I emphasize early memorization because the sooner all the lines are memorized, the better the rehearsals and productions proceed.

It's more important that the kids have a sense of the meaning of their lines than that they memorize them perfectly, word for word. Allow the actors to improvise and paraphrase. When they forget their lines, ask them what their character's intent is at that moment in the story and to describe what is really happening in the story at that point.

FOREIGN LANGUAGE

Whenever possible, ask a native speaker or other expert of the foreign language in the script you're producing to come and work with your cast, helping them learn to pronounce the words correctly, and educating your group about the country or culture being portrayed. Practice speaking the foreign language words together and wherever possible, incorporate them into the rest of your class time together. If you decide that using foreign language will create more rehearsal time than you have available, you can substitute the English translations (alter the Master Script).

CASTING

1. Read or tell the entire story of the play, using either the script or a picture book of the story. Ask the actors to be thinking about which, if any, characters they would most like to play.
2. Ask the actors to say which roles they most prefer and write their choices up on a board where everyone can see them. The actors should name all the roles they most want to play, even if others have named the same roles, or say if they are willing to play any role.
3. Review the list together and work to complete the cast list to everyone's satisfaction.

- *Whenever more than one actor wants the same role, pull names out of a hat to make the decision. I don't recommend the audition process (see below.) The exception here may be to designate that only the older children contend for lead roles that demand a lot of memorization.*
- *Roles can be changed from singular to plural or from plural to singular to accommodate your cast.*
- *The gender of roles can sometimes be changed to accommodate your cast.*

AUDITIONING

Rather than the personal choice and random selection process I recommend above, you can also audition the actors for specific roles. There is certainly something of value in auditioning, but I don't believe it's appropriate for elementary school children, especially the younger ones. At that age, children are more likely to feel "less than" if not chosen than they are to understand the auditioning process. The hurt feelings that often result from auditioning young children work against the goal of building self-esteem and make auditioning both unneccessary and inappropriate.

The personal choice and random selection process of casting accommodates everyone's choices as much as possible and treats everyone equally. The actors' choices of roles can be revealing, while playing them may prove cathartic or otherwise psychologically healing for them.

"COLOR-BLIND" & "GENDER-BLIND" CASTING

"Color-blind" casting is casting roles without regard for, or in conscious defiance of, the race or ethnic heritage of the actors as regards the roles. "Color-blind" casting can create striking, thought-provoking, and even humorous results for it illuminates assumptions about race and raises questions about how we perceive certain roles and ethnic groups.

"Gender-blind" casting does the same thing, with regard to sex role stereotypes. Often, the gender of certain characters is specific for a certain story because the story is passing on important social information about sex roles in that culture (from the past, anyway). It's important to respect all traditions and to only make changes, such as character gender, with purpose—after all, most generations change stories to adapt them to their own time and social values, and our generation can too.

For the sake of simplicity in the scripts, I've labeled each character with gender-specific pronouns and other words ("she/he" gets a bit cumbersome after awhile). These choices are often made randomly— you may change the script as needed. The introductory information for each script indicates which roles can be played as either sex, so that directors can evaluate whether or not the script will work for their particular mix of girls and boys.

Some of your actors may wish to play characters of the opposite sex. You can tell them that this is in keeping with long-standing theater tradition and respectfully accommodate their wishes whenever possible.

BLOCKING

Blocking is the planning of all basic stage placement and movements, and it's the first thing you should do before proceeding with rehearsals. This can be a tedious process, but, is well worth the patience required. Establishing the placement and movement of actors, sets, and props forms a visible framework for the play and helps to focus the work. Pay close attention to all blocking of people and things and keep an accurate record. Each movement affects other parts of the play—a misplaced prop can wreak havoc. All blocking of actors, sets, and props needs to be rehearsed as often as the lines, so it's best to get started early.

During the blocking process it's often difficult for children to pay attention and remain quiet, especially when they're not in the scene being worked on. In the beginning, they often don't understand the "big picture" and where their character fits in. Over the course of rehearsals all the pieces will come together and the play will "jell" for them. Until then, don't expect them to pay total attention when they're not in a scene and set out a quiet activity for them, such as books or drawing materials.

Stage directions are from the perspective of the actors when they're facing the audience; i.e., "right" is the actor's right. "Down" refers to the part of the stage closest to the audience and "up" is the part of the stage farthest from the audience. This is because stages used to be raked, that is, slanted down toward the audience.

AUDIENCE

DOWN LEFT	DOWN CENTER	DOWN RIGHT
LEFT	CENTER	RIGHT
UP LEFT	UP CENTER	UP RIGHT

Use many different levels for your stage, such as tabletops or other platforms, because a variety of levels makes the staging interesting. If the audience is sitting on the same level as the stage, stage your action as high up as possible, especially if the blocking calls for the actors to be sitting or lying down, because the audience in the back rows will have a hard time seeing. Use sturdy tables to your advantage as part of your acting area (and performing on tabletops will also give the kids a thrill.)

Use a lot of exciting action that's fun for the kids and it will be fun for the audience as well. Let them run, jump, skip, fly! Risk a little noise and chaos so that the actors can experience some really exciting movements. Rehearse particularly fast or chaotic action in slow motion first. Always make sure the rules are clear about how to move in the space and in relation with each other so that everyone is safe.

Repetition in blocking helps the actors remember what to do—for example: Their character always enters from a certain place and exits via a certain route. One actor can be assigned to lead group movements, which will make it easy for the others to follow. Sometimes it's useful for the actors to have an assigned order of movement, such as who goes first, second, third, and so forth, because it avoids arguments and helps the kids remember what to do.

When planning blocking, be creative with the furniture you have available. Sturdy tables with folding legs can become slides by folding up one side of the legs. Slides make for interesting movement and are, needless to say, very popular with kids. Tables, chairs, and other furniture can inspire interesting blocking as well as windows, doors, and other built-in features of your room.

Create adequate backstage areas, with enough room for the actors, sets, and props, with places where the actors can watch the play (don't place them where they can't see or hear the play). "Backstage" does not neccessarily mean that the audience can't see the actors. The actors who are not in the current scene can often be included in the scene as onlookers. This will help the kids keep their attention on the play. Make sure you plan the backstage blocking along with the on-stage blocking, so that everyone knows exactly where they're supposed to be at all times.

If you're working with a large cast, create several backstage areas with a different area assigned to each small group of characters. This will go a long way in maintaining order and quiet.

THEATER SPACE

Be creative with your performance space. The following are a few ideas:

- Place the audience around three-quarters of the stage, with you fourth portion being for backdrops, sets, or backstage.

- Create a "theater-in-the-round," where the audience sits in a circle around the stage. The feeling of intimacy can be wonderful and it eliminates the need for large sets or backdrops.
- The entire performance space, including the audience, can be decorated as the setting of the play, so that the audience is made to feel they are "in" the performance.
- Particular aspects of your building can be incorporated into the play setting, such as windows, doors, or closets.
- The performance can take place in various locations which the audience must travel to throughout the course of the play, such as the hallway, other rooms, or outside.

REHEARSALS

Rehearsals should last between thirty minutes to an hour or so. Rehearsals can be alternated with production workshops (making the sets, props, or costumes), or with music rehearsals. Always maintain a rehearsal atmosphere that is positive and fun while being focused and under control.

Be open to new ideas generated by the kids during the first stages of rehearsals. They will most likely come up with great ideas you never thought of, and the actors will feel personally invested in the production if their ideas are heard and, when possible, used. At a certain point, however, you need to establish the artistic decisions so that the play can be rehearsed with consistency and so that everyone can feel secure about it.

After casting and blocking, rehearse individual scenes while creating the production elements (sets, props, and costumes) which are added to rehearsals as they become available. If you don't have all the props available initially, use substitutes so that the actors can get used to them and where they belong. During this time the actors should be memorizing their lines, preferably at home.

The last few rehearsals should be run-throughs of the entire play. As you get close to the performance day, do a few run-throughs that are not interrupted and take notes which you can go over with the cast after the run-through. In addition to your notes, solicit the cast for their comments and suggestions about the run-through.

For one of your last, "dress" rehearsals, invite a preview audience. This will go a long way toward helping your actors focus their attention and get past some of their initial nervousness, as well as "jelling" the play production and working out the "bugs." At the end of this preview performance, ask the cast to sit on the stage while you solicit the audience's questions and comments. You will be amazed at how much a preview performance will improve your production.

If you feel your cast needs a little break from disciplined rehearsals, the following are some ideas for fun, alternative rehearsals, good for when morale is low:

- Rehearse the play in fast-forward. Not only is it extremely silly, it's a good way to drill the lines and blocking.
- Run the lines only, while everyone sits or lies down. A good drill.
- Do the play in gibberish, so that the actors must express their intent through tone of voice, facial expressions, and gestures. Also very silly.
- Switch roles. Seeing what other actors do with their roles can give actors new ideas. If they can't remember the lines exactly, they can paraphrase.

VOCAL PROJECTION

One of the biggest problems in producing plays with kids is getting them to speak loudly, slowly, and clearly. Be strict about vocal projection right from the start because if the audience can't understand the words the whole play will be lost on them.

Help the actors understand that speaking from the stage is not like normal speaking, that it must be louder, slower, and more clearly enunciated. The following are some activities for improving vocal projection:

- Pick a word or phrase from the script and have the actors stand and pretend to put those words in their hands. On the count of 1-2-3, say the words together while pantomiming "throwing" those words across the room and bouncing them off the far wall, as if throwing a ball.
- Practice breathing and good breath control at the beginning of every rehearsal. The diaphragm is a membrane below the lungs which supports good, deep breathing. Show the actors where their diaphragms are located (below the lungs and just above their stomachs) and with your hands on your diaphragms, together practice deep breathing while making your bellies go out on the inhale (the opposite of what

we're used to, which is bellies suck in on the inhale). Together repeat "Ho! Ho! Ho!" or "Sss! Sss! Sss!" while making your bellies jump outward on each syllable, to develop muscle control and awareness of the diaphragm.

Do diction exercises. Here's a few drills (repeat each one over and over):

Topeka

Yamaha

Mama-le, Papa-le

But-a, gut-a

Red leather, yellow leather

B-B-B, B-B-B, BAH! *(and so forth through all the consonants of the alphabet)*

Slippery, southern snakes

Fresh fish, fried fish

You know you need unique New York.

PHYSICAL WARM-UPS

Besides vocal warm-ups, rehearsals should begin with some exercises to loosen up the body, for actors use their whole bodies, not just their voices, to express their characters. A regular discipline of warm-ups helps to focus attention and shift the mood of the group to one of rehearsal concentration. Warm-ups can include stretching, Hatha Yoga postures, and body awareness exercises, such as breathing into each body part, one at a time, and exhaling tension. Always include facial exercises (tongue warm-ups are always a hit).

OTHER EXERCISES & GAMES

When time permits, acting exercises and theater games can augment your rehearsals and help develop skills. They also contribute to a good spirit of group cooperation and add fun to rehearsals. The following are a few ideas:

- One person pantomimes a word, feeling, animal, household task, sport, or other activity while the rest of the group tries to figure out what it is. One variation is to have several ideas under the selected topic written on cards which the actors pick randomly.

- The entire group pantomimes an action, feeling, or sound. The director calls out what it is and the group silently acts it out. This exercise demonstrates that expression is not limited to sound or words.

- All stand in a circle while, one at a time, each person steps into the center, says his name while doing a movement, then steps back into the circle. The whole group together then repeats the name while making the same movement. This is a good activity for learning everyone's names and requires attention in order to mirror each person.

- Get in pairs, each couple facing each other and taking turns doing slow movements while their partner mirrors them. One variation is the director comes around and tries to figure out who is the originator of the movement and who is the mirror, or the whole group can witness each pair and try to figure out who is the originator and who is the mirror. Mirroring is a good exercise for focusing attention.

- All stand in a circle and one person begins by turning her head to the person on the right and saying a word. That person then turns to the person on the right and repeats the word and it continues thus, each person turning to the left to receive the word and to the right to send the word as it goes all around the circle. One variation is to have the director start a second word traveling in the opposite direction.

- All stand in a circle with their eyes closed and hold hands. One person begins to "pass the pulse" by gently squeezing the hand of the person on one side of them. That person continues to pass it and it goes around the circle. One variation is to add a second pulse going the opposite direction. The chief temptation is to start an illegitimate pulse, but if everyone cooperates this exercise can bring the group energy into focus.

- Stand or sit in a circle. The first person tosses a bean bag or rolls a ball to another person anywhere in the circle. That person then tosses it to another person and so forth while everyone keeps track of the order, each person receiving and giving it only once until it makes a complete circuit back to the first person. Continue to repeat this same pattern while adding a second and possibly a third bean bag or ball so that everyone has to stay totally alert at all times.

CHARACTERIZATION

The following are some ideas of ways to encourage the actors to develop their characters:

- From time to time, ask the actors what their character is thinking about or what they want to have happen at that moment in the story.
- Create a mock television interview show and invite each character, one at a time, to the stage to be interviewed by you, the television host, asking them questions about their character, their relationships to other characters, and their actions and intents in the story.
- Improvise scenes between the characters that are not in the play.
- Have the actors write mini-autobiographies of their characters.

MOVEMENT

The following are some ideas of movement activities that can enhance your rehearsals:

- Together as a group, move across the floor as the various characters would move. Ask the actors for words, verbs and adverbs, that describe the movements of each of the characters and all move to express those words.
- One at a time, actors can move across the room as their own character or another actor's character while the group watches and then copies. Actors can get new ideas for their characters by watching other actors move as their character. One variation is for each actor to not say which character is being expressed so that the group has to figure it out by examining the movement.
- Collaborate with a movement teacher who can work with the cast on movement skills and possible choreograph a dance for your show.

CURTAIN CALL & POST-PLAY DISCUSSION

Each actor should be able to take a bow by themselves, perhaps with their name and character announced, to receive their well-deserved applause. Any non-acting stage crew members can also be acknowledged and in the end, the entire cast and crew can take a bow together. Rehearse the bows and maintain onstage quiet and dignity throughout the curtain call, so that everyone gets respect and attention.

After the curtain call, the cast can sit on the stage for a post-play discussion with the audience. The director solicits questions and comments from the audience and facilitates the actors' answers. The actors like to show off and be the experts at this time: Both the curtain call and the post-play discussion are good self-esteem builders.

It's nice to then end the performance with a reception, or "cast party," with snacks and beverages, when the audience and cast can intermingle.

PRODUCTION

The following are some general guidelines for creating all the production elements (sets, props, costumes, and so on):

- Be creative with your resources—you don't have to spend a lot of money on materials. Paper, cardboard, markers, duct tape, and large fabric pieces can take care of most of your needs.
- Duct tape is your best friend—you can even find it in colors other than silver.
- Use the production tasks as activities in creating thinking. While giving the actors practical advice on how to make things, allow them to figure things out and come up with their own ideas for construction and design.
- Prepare each task to be as self-directed as possible. If you thoroughly prepare the materials the actors can work independently and this will free you from the stress of trying to help several groups make things at the same time, or allow you to rehearse with another group simultaneously.
- The directions for making sets, props, costumes, sound, and music listed in the appendixes for each script are only my suggestions—feel free to use other ideas for creating your own, unique production.
- Sets should be simple and light enough for the cast or crew to move themselves. Assign who is to move which set and when and rehearse all the set moves with the rest of the play.
- Props are not toys and should not be played with. They should only be handled by the actor who uses them. These are very important

rules! A missing or broken prop can be devastating in the middle of the play. Have the actors place their own props so they know where they are and always rehearse with props or prop substitutes.

- Create a structure for keeping the props in order backstage (otherwise, kids are often messy with them). Props tables, hooks on the wall, and exact places for each prop are extremely useful and much advised in order to avoid backstage havoc.
- Costumes need not be ornate. The best costumes are often those that the actors create themselves, with colored scarves or other costume props. Plain, black pants and shirts can be embellished with costume pieces that suggest the character, such as a hat, or animals ears and tail.
- If parents sew elaborate costumes they should make them for all the actors so that no child feels outshined. (I personally prefer kid-made costumes.)
- Makeup can be fun but should be optional, for not all children want to wear it. Eye shadow, rouge, and lipstick are easy to get and help bring out the actor's features. Eyebrow pencils are great for mustaches, evil eyebrows, and wicked scars.
- Some children may be allergic to makeup and sharing eye makeup can potentially spread eye diseases such as conjuctivitis (pink eye.) The safest bet is to have actors come with make-up already applied at home.
- "Lights" can be as simple as the switch on the wall. Flicking the lights off and on creates special effects. Table lamps, floor lamps, flashlights, and other lights can be used to create dramatic effects.
- Sound effects can be made with just about anything: percussion instuments, noisemakers, pots and pans...be creative! Tape players can provide music during scene changes which smoothes over the awkward silence while sets are being changed and gives your overall production a classy look.
- Music for songs or dances can be played on tape or CD or played live. If you have time and resources, such as a music teacher, you can create a music ensemble with some of the kids—a "pit orchestra"— to play sound effects and simple percussion.

Preface

I am Vi [taqʷšeblu] Hilbert, Upper Skagit elder, great-grandmother of four and Director of Lushootseed Research.

Because I am the only child of traditional Skagit historians, it has become my responsibility to pass on everything that my culture has taught me to pass on to coming generations of our "first people" (the natives of this country) and to all others who live among us on this land and on this earth.

The old stories of my people were used as our textbooks. They were told to guide us in practicing our age-old values, our history, our geography, our humor, and our memorization (because we had no written languages).

Our historians, those who were willing to have their voices recorded, left valuable information for us in our ancient Lushootseed (Puget Sound Salish) language. Because I have been fortunate enough to learn a writing system for this language, I have been able to bring their words to the printed page in both languages, Lushootseed and in translation to English. Lushootseed Press which I started in 1995 has published these volumes called qʷeqʷulʔe?—Aunt Susie Sampson Peter and siastenu?—Gram Ruth Sehome Shelton. I have also done several other books, two of them were published by the University of Washington Press: an updated *Dictionary of Puget Sound Salish* (1994) and *Haboo*—a book of our literature (1985). In 1980 I self-published another book of our literature also titled *Haboo*. Each of these books contain 33 different stories.

These were textbooks that I used when I taught courses at the University of Washington, 1972–1987. Hundreds of students shared time with me in the classroom. They were from all over the country and there were some exchange students enrolled also from Germany and other countries. We learned from each other!

As an educator and great-grandmother, I feel it is part of my responsibility to accept invitations to lecture to all ages—preschool to senior citizens. It has been gratifying to share information from my culture with international groups also in Europe, Canada, Hawaii and South America.

In London, I was one of forty of the world's recognized storytellers. It was a revelation to some that the oral traditions of our world are indeed the common denominator. We see through our old stories how our wise ancestors taught in parallel fashions.

Pamela Gerke, in using two of the Lushootseed Epic stories to engage very young children in staging productions from another culture, proved to me that the power of our ancient stories can forever be used by all ages and cultures to meet human needs that fulfill those requirements that nurture the spirit of man!

—Vi [taqʷšeblu] Hilbert

Multicultural Plays

for Children

VOLUME I: GRADES K–3

THE ADVENTURES OF ANANSI
(Liberia and Ghana)

These stories from West Africa are in the timeless tradition of the "trickster." Anansi's mischievous counterparts can be found all over the world, such as Coyote and Raven in Native American traditions. Anansi is a popular figure in stories because he's naughty, clever, and full of mischief and yet is loved by everyone—maybe because he reminds us of someone we know, or perhaps ourselves. He loves to eat and hates to work and is always playing tricks on others that get him into a lot of trouble. His saving grace is that he can always laugh at himself and find fun in any situation.

This collection of four Anansi stories can be performed either separately or together and in any order, making this script ideal for working with either a very small cast or with several, small groups. To make this script fairly easy to produce, I've not included any foreign language, songs, or dances.

Anansi can be played by a different actor in each story, and in each, the actor has a lot of lines to memorize. Story #2, "How Anansi Helped a Fisherman" requires two actors who can memorize a lot of lines. In three of the stories there can be numerous Villagers, many whom can have nonspeaking roles. Spread out the Villagers lines as needed. As in all the plays in this book, the part of the Narrator can be distributed over several speakers, thus creating more speaking parts.

RUNNING TIME OF SHOW: (*approximate*)
6-10 minutes per story; 25-30 minutes total

REHEARSAL TIME NEEDED:
3-5 hours per story; 10-12 hours total

OTHER PRODUCTION TIME NEEDED:
2-4 hours total

CAST SIZE:
Minimum/Maximum:
#1: 5, plus Narrator (only 2 Villagers)/9-12 (6-9 Villagers)
#2: 4, plus Narrator (only 2 Villagers)/8-10 (6-8 Villagers)
#3: 2, plus Narrator/same
#4: 5, plus Narrator/10+ (numerous People & Animals)
Total show: 5, plus Narrator/25-30

GENDER OF CHARACTERS:
In stories #1 and #4, Anansi is referred to as "father" by his "sons" but it may be possible to reverse the genders; otherwise, all characters, including Anansi, can be played as either female or male.

Play #1: "How Anansi Got A Thin Waist"

CHARACTERS:
NARRATOR
ANANSI
KUMA – Anansi's son
KWAKU – Anansi's son
VILLAGERS (2 – 6 or more)

(Setting: The forest near Anansi's village in West Africa. There may be a forest backdrop and/or tree and bush sets which can serve for all four stories. For the other stories, there will need to be a river set, a market-place, Anansi's house, possibly a tree or bush set, and a climbable tree set – see each story for descriptions of sets. Backstage on one side is a long rope. The middle of the rope is tied in a loop, big enough to fit around Anansi's waist; the loop will get smaller when both ends of the rope are pulled. LIGHTS UP.)

NARRATOR: Long ago in West Africa, Anansi the Spider did not look like he does today. Of course, he had eight legs and lived in a web, but back then, he was big all over and his waistline was very fat. Today he still has a big head and a big body but with a thin waist and this is how it came to pass:
One day, Anansi was walking through the forest when he smelled something wonderful.

(ANANSI enters. His shirt is stuffed with pillows to make his waist look very fat.)

ANANSI: *(Sniffing the air.)* FOOD!!! Why, I'd almost forgotten – today is the harvest festival and everyone in the villages is preparing for a feast!

(VILLAGERS enter, talking to each other.)

VILLAGER #1: I'm cooking yams and cassava, and chicken with peanut-flavored sauce!
VILLAGER #2: I'm preparing fish and peppers, and rice boiling in a great big pot over the fire!
ANANSI: *(Eagerly.)* Can I come to the feast?
VILLAGER #3: No! You haven't done any work to prepare for it!

VILLAGER #4: You didn't plant yams or potatoes or rice!
VILLAGER #5: You didn't go out to sea to catch fish!
ANANSI: But I don't like to work!
VILLAGER #6: You're disgusting!

(VILLAGERS look disgusted with him and exit. ANANSI sits down.)

NARRATOR: It was true, Anansi played or slept all day and never worked. And since it's the custom to never refuse to feed anyone who comes to your house, Anansi ate very well by simply visiting all his friends. In fact, he ate more than they did, which explains why his waist was so fat.

Anansi got more and more hungry as he smelled all the good food being prepared in the villages.

ANANSI: *(Standing.)* There's a village in the east *(Points to one side of the stage.)* and another village in the west *(Points to the other side.)* …Which feast should I go to?

… I know! I'll go to both of them!

But how will I know when the food is ready? … I know!

(He does a little dance for joy.)

ANANSI: *(Calling out.)* KUMA!!! Come here!

(KUMA enters. ANANSI gets rope.)

KUMA: Yes, father?
ANANSI: Take this rope to the village in the east. When the food is ready, give the rope a hard pull and then I'll know it's time for me to come and eat!
KUMA: Yes, father.

(ANANSI gives him one end of the rope and KUMA exits to one side of the stage. ANANSI slips the rope loop around his waist.)

ANANSI: *(Calling out.)* KWAKU!!! Come here!

(KWAKU enters.)

KWAKU: Yes, father?
ANANSI: Take this rope to the village in the west. When the food is ready, give the rope a hard pull and then I'll know it's time for me to come and eat!

KWAKU: Yes, father.

(ANANSI gives him the other end of the rope and KWAKU exits to the other side of the stage.)

NARRATOR: Can you guess what happened? The people in the east village and the people in the west village had their dinners at *exactly the same time!*

(KUMA & KWAKU simultaneously give a pull on the rope. ANANSI cries out in alarm and struggles to go one direction or another, but can't.)

KUMA & KWAKU: *(Simultaneously.)* Why hasn't father come to the feast yet? I'd better pull harder!

(They pull on the rope again while ANANSI jerks around, crying out in alarm while being pulled this way and that.)

KUMA & KWAKU: *(Simultaneously.)* He *still* isn't here! I'd better pull even harder!

(They continue to pull on the rope while ANANSI jerks around, crying out in alarm while surreptitiously pulling the pillows out of his shirt when his back is toward the audience.)

NARRATOR: Anansi was never fat again. He stayed the same until today, with his fat head and fat body and thin, little waist in between.

(KUMA and KWAKU let go of rope and Anansi lets it fall to the floor.)

ANANSI: *(Admiring his waist.)* How thin I am! Now I'll have to eat more to fatten up! *(ANANSI exits, skipping merrily)*

(LIGHTS DOWN.)

Play #2: "How Anansi Helped a Fisherman"

CHARACTERS:
NARRATOR
ANANSI
FISHERMAN
VILLAGERS (two or more)

(Setting: A fishing village in West Africa. The stage can be set as for the other stories. There is a river in one area of the stage, represented by either a long, blue cloth laid on the floor or by a freestanding cardboard wall decorated as the river. In or behind the river set are nets full of several, large fish, plus some extra fish. In another area of the stage is the village marketplace, indicated by barrels, boxes, and/or goods for sale or possibly a freestanding wall painted as the market scene. Nearby are the fish traps, which can be net bags. LIGHTS UP.)

NARRATOR: In the village of Akim there once was a hardworking fisherman.

(FISHERMAN enters with a large bag, pulls nets out of the river and unloads fish into the bag.)

NARRATOR: Everyday, he gathered his nets of fish and brought them to market.

(VILLAGERS enter marketplace as FISHERMAN goes there. They pantomime buying and selling the fish.)

NARRATOR: When he wasn't setting his fish traps, or gathering his fish and selling them, the Fisherman was mending his nets and cleaning his boat. Anansi noticed how hard the fisherman worked and we know that Anansi could not stand hard work.

(ANANSI enters and watches the Fisherman in the marketplace.)

NARRATOR: But Anansi also noticed how many big fish the Fisherman brought to market each day and what a feast the Fisherman's family had every night. Anansi decided to play a trick on the Fisherman so that he could get some of the fish for himself.

ANANSI: *(To Fisherman:)* Hello! May I help you with your work?

FISHERMAN: Of course! I'd be very glad to have your help!

VILLAGER #1: *(Laughing, to other Villagers:)* That Fisherman is a fool!

VILLAGER #2: He'll end up doing all the work but Anansi will get all the fish!

(FISHERMAN overhears them and smiles slyly.)

FISHERMAN: *(To himself:)* We shall see about that ...

(VILLAGERS exit.)

FISHERMAN: *(To ANANSI:)* This is how we will do things: someone has to do the work and someone has to get tired, so we'll take turns. Today, I'll make the fish traps and *you* will get tired.

ANANSI: I, get tired?!! No way! I'll make the fish traps and *you* will be the one who gets tired!

FISHERMAN: ...Very well, if that's what you want... *(Yawns.)* Oh, I'm *so* tired!

(FISHERMAN lays down and snores while ANANSI gets out the traps and pantomimes working on them. LIGHTS DOWN. LIGHTS UP.)

NARRATOR: The next day, the Fisherman said:

FISHERMAN: My friend, yesterday you made the traps and I got tired. Today we'll switch – I'll set the traps in the river and *you* will get tired.

ANANSI: I, get tired?!! No way! I'll set the traps and *you* will be the one who gets tired!

FISHERMAN: ...Very well, if that's what you want... *(Yawns.)* Oh, I'm *so* tired!

(They go to the river and FISHERMAN lays down and snores while ANANSI sets the traps in the river. LIGHTS DOWN. LIGHTS UP.)

NARRATOR: The next day the Fisherman said:

FISHERMAN: My friend, yesterday you set the traps and I got tired. Today we'll switch – I'll collect the fish in the traps and *you* will get tired.

ANANSI: I, get tired?!! No way! I'll collect the fish and *you* will be the one who gets tired!

FISHERMAN: ...Very well, if that's what you want... *(Yawns.)* Oh, I'm *so* tired!

(FISHERMAN lays down and snores while ANANSI pulls the traps

out of the river with fish in them. A backstage person has stuffed the traps or, if using a cloth as a river set, ANANSI can simply fill up the bags with fish that are laying under the cloth. LIGHTS DOWN. LIGHTS UP.)

NARRATOR: The next day the Fisherman said:

FISHERMAN: My friend, yesterday you collected the fish and I got tired. Today we'll switch – I'll take the fish to the market to sell and *you* will get tired.

ANANSI: Do you think I'm a fool?!! I will *never* agree to get tired! I'll take the fish to the market to sell and *you* will be the one who gets tired!

FISHERMAN: …Very well, if that's what you want… *(Yawns.)* Oh, I'm *so* tired!

(They go to the marketplace, FISHERMAN yawning and ANANSI carrying all the fish. Meanwhile, VILLAGERS enter the marketplace. ANANSI sells the fish to the VILLAGERS, who give their money to FISHERMAN – actors can ad lib the buying and selling until all the fish are gone.)

FISHERMAN: *(To ANANSI:)* Thanks for helping me. Here's four coins for you.

(FISHERMAN gives coins to ANANSI then exits. ANANSI stares at the coins.)

ANANSI: *(Angry.)* I've been tricked!!

(VILLAGERS all laugh. ANANSI stares at them for a moment then smiles.)

ANANSI: Oh, well! Next time, I'll be the winner!

(ANANSI exits, skipping and laughing.)

VILLAGER #3: The one who plays tricks may himself be tricked if he's too greedy!

(LIGHTS DOWN.)

Play #3: "Why Anansi Lives in Ceilings"

CHARACTERS
NARRATOR
ANANSI
LEOPARD

(Setting: Anansi's house. The stage can be set as for the other stories. ANANSI'S house is a hut made of banana leaves and is made of a sturdy table with either a cloth hanging down the front or with a free-standing cardboard wall decorated as the front of the house set in front of the table. There is a stepladder or chair next to or behind the table so that ANANSI can climb to the "rooftop." Nearby there is a tree, bush, or other set for ANANSI to hide behind – this could be the tree from Story #4 or other set, such as the reverse side of the river set. LIGHTS UP.)

NARRATOR: Every year the rainy season comes to the forest. But one year there was more rain than ever before. It fell from the sky in a big flood, day after day, and all the animals could do was shiver under trees or in caves, unable to go out and seek food. All the animals became very hungry, especially Anansi, who, as usual, had been too lazy to plant his farm or set his fish traps and so had nothing at all to eat. One afternoon the rain finally stopped. Anansi set out at once to look for some food.

(ANANSI comes out of his house and looks around.)

NARRATOR: During this time the great Leopard, who normally hunts at night, was so hungry that she had to stalk the forest during the daytime.

(LEOPARD enters.)

LEOPARD: *(Too sweetly.)* Good afternoon, Anansi! How are you doing in all this rain?
ANANSI: *(Suspiciously.)* I'm well, Leopard ... but I'm in a great hurry!

(ANANSI jumps behind a tree or bush. LEOPARD is angry and tries to find him, swiping the air with her claws, but cannot.)

LEOPARD: *(Roaring.)* Where did he go?!! ... Never mind. I'll go to Anansi's house and wait for him to come back. Then I'll eat him!

(LEOPARD goes into ANANSI'S house. ANANSI comes out of hiding and exits.)

NARRATOR: Anansi was not stupid – he figured out that Leopard was hungry enough to eat even a little spider. Anansi stalled around all day, looking for any of his friends who could possibly feed him, and staying away from his house for as long as he could. Finally it began to get dark and once again the rain began to fall. Anansi had to go home.

(ANANSI enters, cautiously. Then he assumes a casual pose and begins to whistle or hum loudly. When he comes close to his house, he stops.)

ANANSI: *(Calling out.)* Hello, my banana-leaf house!! *(Pause, then loudly.)* That's funny, my little house always answers me when I call her! I wonder what's the matter?!! *(Calling out.)* Hello, my banana-leaf house!!
LEOPARD: *(In a small, high voice from inside the house.)* Hello, Anansi! Come on in!
ANANSI: *(Laughing.)* Now I know where you are, Leopard! And you shall never catch me!

(ANANSI scampers up to the roof of his house. LEOPARD comes out of the house, growling and swiping at him with her claws, but ANANSI is out of her reach. Actors ad lib ANANSI taunting her and LEOPARD trying to get him.)

NARRATOR: Leopard never could catch Anansi, who was warm and dry and safe on the ceiling. I suppose that's why he decided to live up there. And Anansi, the spider, is still living there.

(LIGHTS DOWN.)

Play #4: "How The World Got Wisdom"

CHARACTERS:
NARRATOR
ANANSI
NYAME – the Sky God
TORTOISE
HARE
KUMA – Anansi's son
PEOPLE & ANIMALS

(Setting: Anansi's house, as before. In another area of the stage is a large, climbable tree set, made of a slide or other furniture, decorated as a tree with leaves and branches at the top but none at the bottom. There may possibly be a large, cardboard replica of the tree placed in front of or next to the slide. In another area of the stage is a raised platform, such as a table or chair, for NYAME to stand on. LIGHTS UP.)

NARRATOR: What is wisdom? Some say it's another word for good sense. Nowadays there's wisdom everywhere in the world, but there wouldn't be any at all if it hadn't been for Anansi's accident. Once, when the world was very new, Nyame, the Sky God, called to Anansi.

(NYAME enters and stands on raised platform. She holds a bag full of small candies, toys or party favors – the "wisdom." The bag has a handle large enough to slip over Anansi's head. In the original story, Anansi puts the "wisdom" in a clay pot which later breaks into many pieces but it's easier and safer to stage if the "wisdom" is spilled from a bag.)

NYAME: *(Calling out.)* ANANSI!!

(ANANSI comes out of his house.)

ANANSI: Yes, Nyame?
NYAME: Here's all the wisdom in the world! Do whatever you want with it!

(NYAME gives ANANSI the bag. NYAME can then either exit or watch the rest of the play from her perch.)

ANANSI: I'm so lucky to have all this wisdom! Since I'm the only one with any wisdom, I could rule the world! I'd better hide it so nobody else can have it!

(ANANSI quickly runs into his house to put away the bag. Meanwhile, HARE & TORTOISE enter together and cross the stage. ANANSI comes out of his house.)

TORTOISE: Where are you going, Anansi?
HARE: Why are you in such a hurry?

(ANANSI hurries past them.)

TORTOISE: Sister Hare, I suspect that Anansi must be into some mischief again!
HARE: Brother Tortoise, I think you're right!
TORTOISE: Hey, I have an idea! Let's have a race!
HARE: Okay!

(They exit. ANANSI goes to the big tree and looks up it.)

ANANSI: This tree is the perfect hiding place! No one will be able to climb it because there's no branches near the ground!

(ANANSI goes back to his house, gets the bag, and hurries back to the tree. He pulls the bag handle over his head so that the bag hangs in front of him. He begins to climb the tree but has great difficulty as the bag is very heavy and gets in his way. Whenever he gets part of the way up the tree he slips and falls to the ground.)

ANANSI: With my eight legs, surely I can climb this tree!

(He keeps trying and failing to climb the tree, getting more and more frustrated- actor may ad lib lines. KUMA enters and watches.)

KUMA: Father, I have an idea! If you hang the bag behind you instead of in front of you, you'll be better able to climb the tree.
ANANSI: *(Angry.)* Kuma! You must have some wisdom, too!! Which means that I don't have all the wisdom in the world for myself! AARRGGHH!!!

(ANANSI, in a fit of temper, throws the bag to the ground so that all the "wisdom" spills out all over the floor.)

NARRATOR: People and animals came from all around to gather the wisdom.

(PEOPLE & ANIMALS enter, pick up the "wisdom" and give it to audience members.)

NARRATOR: They spread it all over the world. There was plenty to go around!

ANANSI: Plenty for you and plenty for me!

ALL: The end!

(LIGHTS DOWN.)

APPENDIX A: VOCABULARY LIST OF FOREIGN LANGUAGE

(not applicable)

APPENDIX B: SETS

SETS LIST

ALL STORIES:
  forest backdrop (optional)
  freestanding trees and bushes (optional)

#2 – RIVER:
  freestanding wall OR long, blue cloth

MARKETPLACE:
  barrels, boxes, goods for sale AND/OR freestanding wall of market scene

#3 & #4 – ANANSI'S HOUSE:
  1 table
  cloth, tape OR free-standing wall
  1 stepladder, chair or other access to tabletop

#4 – TREE:
  1 slide or other climbable furniture, decorated with leaves and branches
  large, cardboard replica of tree (optional)

HOW TO MAKE THE SETS

FREESTANDING WALLS (for trees, bushes, forest backdrop, river, marketplace and Anansi's house)
- very large cardboard box
- cardboard cutting knife
- scissors
- heavy butcher paper
- tape or glue
- markers, crayons or paint with brushes
- colored paper or fabric (optional)

Cut box to create a freestanding wall with accordion folds. Cut butcher paper to size of the wall. Tape or glue paper to one or both sides of the wall (if cardboard is plain white, you can eliminate this step). River or marketplace sets could have forest backdrop or Anansi's house on the reverse sides. River set can have a hatch for passing the fish traps through. (To make the hatch, draw a square somewhere in the middle of the wall, large enough for the net bags of fish to pass through. Cut sides and bottom of square and fold up top to create a hatch door.) Draw picture of the set on the wall with markers, crayons, or paint. Colored paper or fabric can also be used to decorate the wall, using glue or tape. Anansi's house is covered with large, green or brown paper leaves to represent banana leaves.

LANDSCAPE BACKDROP
- heavy butcher paper
- markers, crayons or paint with brushes
- sturdy tape
- scissors

Cut butcher paper to fit across upstage wall. Draw scenes of the forest with markers, crayons, or paint. Make sure the artists understand which end is up and that drawings must be large enough to be seen from the audience. Tape to wall.

APPENDIX C: PROPS

PROPS LIST

#1: Pillows (for Anansi's fat stomach)
    Long Rope
#2: Net Bags (fish traps and fish carrying bags)
    Fish (paper or plastic)
    4 Coins
    Marketing Props (optional, for Villagers)
#4 Large Bag (with handle big enough to slip over Anansi's head)

Wisdom (candies, toys or party favors, enough for all the audience and cast members)

COSTUMES LIST

ANANSI: plain, black pants & shirt or leotard & tights (plus shoes if the floor is too slippery for tights)

KUMA, KWAKU, VILLAGERS & FISHERMAN: traditional West African dress, or plain clothes with African cloth draped around waists, shoulders or heads, and bare feet

LEOPARD: leopard costume or plain, brown or yellow pants & shirt or leotard & tights, with ears and tail

TORTOISE: plain, green pants & shirt or leotard & tights, possibly with turtle shell

HARE: plain white, brown, black or gray pants & shirt or leotard & tights, with ears and tail (tail can be a piece of fake fur, pinned on)

NYAME: fanciful "Sky God" costume, such as a decorated gown, glittery head piece, and so on

HOW TO MAKE THE COSTUMES

EARS (for Leopard and Hare)
- colored construction paper
- pencil
- scissors
- stapler
- light cardboard, glue (optional)
- markers, crayons, paint with brushes, (optional)
- fake fur, glue (optional)

Draw and cut out shape of animal ears with pencil on appropriate color of paper. Cut a long strip of the same color, approximately 4 cm wide and long enough to go around the actor's head with 2-3 centimeters of overlap. Staple ears to strip, and staple strips to fit snugly around the actor's head. You may want to reinforce ears and strips with a cardboard backing. Decorate as needed with markers, crayons, paint, or bits of fake fur.

LEOPARD TAIL
- long strips, approx. 1 meter long, of colored chiffon or other light fabric
- scissors
- long, elastic strip or safety pins

Measure out three strips of fabric. Braid together and tie in a knot at either end. Tail is either pinned to back of actor's pants or tied to an elastic strip that is measured and tied to fit around actor's waist. The best place to pin the tail to pants is through belt loops. If you pin it directly to pants or shirt, it can rip the fabric if someone steps on the tail.

APPENDIX E: SOUND & MUSIC

MUSIC: West African music to play between stories, played live or on tape or CD

DRAKESBILL
(France)

This old tale shows us that it helps to have a few friends in your mouth. The play has a lot of fun, exciting action in it and a giant duck's mouth set. If you can have a slide coming out of this set, it makes for a marvelous effect as the various friends of Drakesbill come sliding out and to the rescue. There's French language and a French folksong included.

RUNNING TIME OF SHOW: (*approximate*)
20-25 minutes

REHEARSAL TIME NEEDED:
8-10 hours

OTHER PRODUCTION TIME NEEDED:
4-6 hours

CAST SIZE:
Minimum: 10, plus Narrator (The bank scene can be played by actors playing other roles and there can be a minimum of 2 King's Servants & Guards and 2 Chickens & Turkeys, who also play Flames, Wasps, and People.)

Maximum: 25-30 (The River can be played by several people and there can be numerous Bank Customers, King's Servants & Guards, Chickens & Turkeys, Wasps, Flames, and People.)

GENDER OF CHARACTERS:
All roles can be played as either female or male, and the King can be played as a Queen.

CHARACTERS:

NARRATOR
DRAKESBILL – a duck
BANK TELLER
AGENT - for Le Roi
BANK CUSTOMERS (optional)
RENARD – fox
RIVIÈRE – river (1 or more actors)
ÉCHELLE – ladder
NID DES GUÊPES – wasp-nest
GUÊPES – wasps

LE ROI (or LA REINE) King
  or Queen
SERVANTS & GUARDS:
  DOORKEEPER
  GUARDS
  OTHER SERVANTS (opt.)
  CHICKENS & TURKEYS
  FLAMES (optional)
  PEOPLE (optional)

SCENE 1

(Setting: A bank. There is a bank counter and there can be other bank accoutrements, such as chairs and signs. BANK TELLER enters and stands behind the counter. BANK CUSTOMERS enter and either stand in line at the counter or mill about while AGENT stands or sits nearby. There can also be additional tellers or other bank personnel. LIGHTS UP. DRAKESBILL enters, quacking, and gets in line at the counter. BANK TELLER & CUSTOMERS can ad lib bank transactions until DRAKESBILL reaches the front of the line.)

TELLER: *Bonjour, Monsieur* Drakesbill!

DRAKESBILL: QUACK!! *Bonjour!*

TELLER: Another deposit, *Monsieur* Drakesbill? My, your savings account is enormous!

AGENT: (*Overhearing.*) *Pardonez-moi, Monsieur* Drakesbill. I am the agent for *le Roi*, the King. How would you like the great privilege of loaning your money to *le Roi?*

DRAKESBILL: *Oui!* I'd be honored!

KING'S AGENT: (*To Teller:*) You heard the duck – transfer all his savings to the King's account!

TELLER: *Oui!*

(LIGHTS DOWN. Change set: ALL exit.)

SCENE 2

(Setting: The countryside, on the way to the King's Palace. The stage is basically bare except for a giant replica of a duck's face, created by a freestanding wall with a hatchway into the mouth through the bills. This is set on a sturdy table with a slide placed below the mouth and pointed toward at the audience. In lieu of a sturdy table and slide, the duck's face can be set on the floor. For now, the duck's face is covered with a plain cloth. RENARD, ÉCHELLE, RIVIÈRE & NID DES GUÊPES are backstage and will come onstage at various places along DRAKESBILL'S route. LIGHTS UP.)

NARRATOR: A year went by...two years, three years...and *le Roi*, who never did anything but spend money, made no offer to repay the loan from Drakesbill. At last the duck made up his mind to go and see *le Roi* and try to get his money back.

(DRAKESBILL enters.)

DRAKESBILL:
Quack, quack, quack! I wanna get my money back!
Coin, coin, coin! L'argent j'en ai besoin!

(RENARD enters.)

RENARD: *Bonjour!*
DRAKESBILL: *Bonjour, Renard!* Hello, Fox!
RENARD: *Où allez-vous?*
DRAKESBILL: I'm going to ask *le Roi* to pay me what he owes me.
RENARD: Oh, take me with you, *s'il vous plaît!*
DRAKESBILL: (*Thinks a moment.*) Hmm...*Oui, mon ami!* But you will soon get tired. Make yourself very small, climb into my mouth, and I will carry you!
RENARD: *Merci beaucoup!*

(SOUND & LIGHTS EFFECTS as cloth is removed from the duck's face and RENARD climbs up the slide and into the mouth. DRAKES-BILL continues on his journey. ÉCHELLE enters.)

DRAKESBILL:
Quack, quack, quack! I wanna get my money back!
Coin, coin, coin! L'argent j'en ai besoin!
ÉCHELLE: *Bonjour!*
DRAKESBILL: *Bonjour, Échelle!* Hello, Ladder!
ÉCHELLE: *Où allez-vous?*
DRAKESBILL: I'm going to ask *le Roi* to pay me what he owes me.
ÉCHELLE: Oh, take me with you, *s'il vous plaît!*
DRAKESBILL: (*Thinks a moment.*) Hmm...*Oui, mon ami!* But you will soon get tired. Make yourself very small, climb into my mouth, and I will carry you!
ÉCHELLE: *Merci beaucoup!*

(SOUND & LIGHTS EFFECTS as ÉCHELLE climbs up the slide and into the mouth. DRAKESBILL continues on his journey. RIVIÈRE enters, trailing a long, blue cloth.)

DRAKESBILL:
Quack, quack, quack! I wanna get my money back!
Coin, coin, coin! L'argent j'en ai besoin!
RIVIERE: *Bonjour!*
DRAKESBILL: *Bonjour,* Rivière! Hello, River!
RIVIERE: *Où allez-vous?*
DRAKESBILL: I'm going to ask *le Roi* to pay me what he owes me.
RIVIERE: Oh, take me with you, *s'il vous plâit!*
DRAKESBILL: (*Thinks a moment.*) Hmm ... *Oui, mon ami!* But you
will soon get tired. Make yourself very small, climb into my
mouth, and I will carry you!
RIVIERE: *Merci beaucoup!*

*(SOUND & LIGHTS EFFECTS as RIVIÈRE climbs up the slide
and into the mouth. DRAKESBILL continues on his journey. NID
DES GUÊPES enters, surrounded by GUÊPES.)*

DRAKESBILL:
Quack, quack, quack! I wanna get my money back!
Coin, coin, coin! L'argent j'en ai besoin!
NID DES GUÊPES: *Bonjour!*
DRAKESBILL: *Bonjour, Nid des Guêpes!* Hello, Wasp-nest!
NID DES GUÊPES: *Où allez-vous?*
DRAKESBILL: I'm going to ask *le Roi* to pay me what he owes me.
NID DES GUÊPES: Oh, take me with you, *s'il vous plâit!*
DRAKESBILL: (*Thinks a moment.*) Hmm...*Oui, mon ami!* But you
will soon get tired. Make yourself very small, climb into my
mouth, and I will carry you!
NID DES GUÊPES: Merci beaucoup!

*(SOUND & LIGHTS EFFECTS as NID DES GUÊPES &
GUÊPES climb up the slide and into the mouth.)*

DRAKESBILL: Quack, quack, quack! I wanna get my money back!

*(DRAKESBILL exits. LIGHTS DOWN. Bring in Castle set, leave
duck's mouth in place.)*

SCENE 3

*(Setting: The King's Castle. In one area is the throne room, set with
one throne and possibly a freestanding wall or other backdrop of throne*

room interior. LE ROI is on his throne and his AGENT is by his side. GUARDS are standing nearby, as are other SERVANTS and PEO-PLE. In another area is the poultry yard with a gate, represented by a freestanding wall, one end of which can swing open and shut. In another area is the well, made out of a large barrel or cardboard box. There is a stepladder or chair behind the well upstage and another inside of the well, so that the actor can easily climb in and out. There are some blue fabric pieces inside the well, to represent water. There is a freestanding "fire" set backstage, including hatches through which to wave fire-colored tissue paper or fabric. CHICKENS & TURKEYS are backstage behind the poultry yard, FLAMES are backstage with the fire set, and behind the duck's mouth are RENARD, ÉCHELLE, RIVIÈRE,GUÊPES & NID DES GUÊPES. LIGHTS UP. DRAKES-BILL enters, goes up to the castle door and knocks: SOUND EFFECT. DOORKEEPER enters and comes to the door.)

DOORKEEPER: *Oui?*
DRAKESBILL: *Je m'appelle* Drakesbill. I want to speak with *le Roi!*

(DOORKEEPER goes to LE ROI.)

DOORKEEPER: Your majesty, there's someone here to see you named Drakesbill.
LE ROI: Who?!!
AGENT: That's the duck you borrowed all the money from.
LE ROI: Oh ... Throw him in with the chickens and turkeys!

(DOORKEEPER goes back to DRAKESBILL.)

DOORKEEPER: Follow me!

(DOORKEEPER leads DRAKESBILL to the poultry yard and then slams and locks the door behind him. CHICKENS & TURKEYS enter, clucking and gobbling, and attack him. DRAKESBILL tries frantically to escape.)

DRAKESBILL:
Renard, Renard, from beneath my tongue,
Come quick or soon my song will be sung!

(RENARD jumps out of the duck's mouth and chases away the CHICKENS & TURKEYS. DRAKESBILL goes directly to the King.)

DRAKESBILL:
Quack, quack, quack! I wanna get my money back!
Coin, coin, coin! L'argent j'en ai besoin!
LE ROI: WHAT?!! GUARDS!! Throw the duck in the well!

(GUARDS rush to DRAKESBILL, grab him and throw him in the well. DRAKESBILL frantically bobs up and down as if he is drowning while throwing the blue fabric pieces up into the air to represent water splashing.)

DRAKESBILL:
Échelle, Échelle, from beneath my tongue,
Come quick or soon my song will be sung!

(ÉCHELLE jumps out of the duck's mouth and rushes over to the well. ÉCHELLE stands behind the well upstage and places it's lower rungs into the well. DRAKESBILL, using the stepladder or chair inside the well, climbs out. If ÉCHELLE stands in the same proximity, it will look as if DRAKESBILL is climbing ÉCHELLE. DRAKESBILL goes directly to LE ROI.)

DRAKESBILL:
Quack, quack, quack! I wanna get my money back!
Coin, coin, coin! L'argent j'en ai besoin!
LE ROI: WHAT?!! GUARDS! Throw the duck in a big fire!

(GUARDS grab DRAKESBILL while SERVANTS build a large fire. This can be simulated by either a fire set and/or FLAME actors who leap and dance about. The GUARDS prepare to throw DRAKESBILL into the fire while he struggles, panic-stricken.)

DRAKESBILL:
Rivière, Rivière, from beneath my tongue,
Come quick or soon my song will be sung!

(RIVIÈRE jumps out of the duck's mouth, rushes over to the fire and spreads it's long, blue cloth over it, putting it out. The water continues to fill up the castle, simulated by more long, blue cloths which are carried onstage and spread over everything. SERVANTS & GUARDS struggle to keep from drowning and LE ROI stands on his throne while DRAKESBILL easily swims around.)

DRAKESBILL:
Quack, quack, quack! I wanna get my money back!
Coin, coin, coin! L'argent j'en ai besoin!
LE ROI: GUARDS!! Seize the duck and bring him to me! I will kill him!
DRAKESBILL:
Guêpes, Guêpes, from beneath my tongue!
Come quick or soon my song will be sung!

(GUÊPES come charging out of the duck's mouth.)

GUÊPES: CHARGE!!!

(They chase LE ROI & GUARDS from the castle. The PEOPLE of the castle enter.)

PEOPLE: *Le Roi* is dead! Long live our new king!

(They place a crown on DRAKESBILL who sits on the throne. The next lines can be re-assigned to other characters if needed.)

PEOPLE: Hooray!
PERSON #1: He doesn't look like *le Roi!*
PERSON #2: A duck is better than a king who does nothing but spend our money!
PEOPLE: SPEECH! SPEECH!
DRAKESBILL: Ladies and gentlemen: I am very hungry. Let's eat!

(May have song/dance here: "L'Autre Jour en Voulant Danser" or other French folksong.)

ALL: *C'est fini!* The end!

(LIGHTS DOWN)

APPENDIX A: VOCABULARY LIST OF FOREIGN LANGUAGE

FRENCH	ENGLISH	PRONUNCIATION
bonjour	good day, hello	bohn-jhoor'
c'est fini	it is finished, the end	say fin-ee'
Coin, coin, coin! L'argent j'en ai besoin! ("Coin" is how the French say what a duck says)	Quack, quack, quack! The money is what I need!	kwa, kwa, kwa * lahr-jhah' ** jhon-aye' biz-wa' *
échelle	ladder	aye-shell'
guêpes, nid des guêpes	wasps, wasp-nest	gwep, nee day gwep
je m'appelle	my name is ("I am called")	juh mah-pell' (soft "j")
le roi / la reine	the king / the queen	luh r'wah' / lah rehne' +
monsieur / madame	mister / madam	muss-yeur' / mah-dahm'
merci beaucoup	thank you very much	mare-see bow-koo' +
mon ami	my friend	mohn ah-mee'
Où allez-vous?	Where are you going?	Oo' ah-lay-voo'?
oui	yes	wee
pardonez-moi	pardon me, excuse me	pahr-dohn-eh mwah'
renard	fox	ruh-nahr'
rivière	river	rih-vee-y'air'
s'il vous plâit	please	see voo play'

* *"a" as in "add"*
** *"jhah" sounds halfway between "oh" and "ah", in back of the throat*
\+ *French "r" is sounded in the back of the throat, gutturally*

"L'Autre Jour En Voulant Danser" (song):
L'autre jour en voulant danser
While I was dancing the other day
loh'-truh jhoor ah(n)' voo-lah(n)' dahn-say'

gai fa-ri-ra, la-ri-ra dondé, dondaine
Old French, idiomatic for "tra-la-la", etc.
g'eye fa-ree-rah', lah-ree-rah' dawn-day', dawn-day'-nuh

Une épine entra dans mon soulier (hou, hou, and so on)
Something sharp (a spine) stuck in my shoe (ha, ha, and so on)
oon eh-peen' ehn-trah' moh(n) soo-lee-ay' (hoo, hoo, and so on)

SETS LIST

BANK:
> 1-2 tables
> chairs (optional)
> bank signs (optional)

DUCK'S MOUTH:
> freestanding wall of mouth with large hatchway
> 1-2 large, sturdy tables
> slide or other access to/from duck's mouth
> large, plain cloth

THRONE ROOM:
> 1 chair
> freestanding wall or other backdrop

POULTRY YARD:
> freestanding wall, including gate

WELL:
> large barrel or cardboard box
> 2 chairs or stepladders
> blue fabric pieces

FIRE
> freestanding wall with small hatches
> fire-colored tissue paper or fabric

FLOOD:
> long blue fabric pieces

HOW TO MAKE THE SETS

FREESTANDING WALLS (for throne room interior, duck's mouth, poultry yard and fire)
- very large cardboard box
- cardboard cutting knife
- scissors
- heavy butcher paper
- tape or glue
- markers, crayons or paint with brushes
- colored paper or fabric (optional)

Cut box to create a freestanding wall with accordian folds. The duck's mouth will need a big hatchway in the center, large enough for the actors to move through *(The duck bills can be painted 2-D, or you can create 3-D bills). The fire set will need small hatches here and there through which to wave fire-colored tissue paper or fabric. To cut hatches, draw a square on the cardboard, large enough for the intended objects. Duck's mouth hatch should be from about the middle of the wall to the floor. Cut sides and bottom of square and fold up top to create a hatch door. Cut a piece of butcher paper to size of the wall. Tape or glue paper to the wall, including any hatches (if cardboard is plain white, you can eliminate this step). Draw picture of the set on the wall with markers, crayons, or paint. Colored paper or fabric can also be used to decorate the wall, using glue or tape.*

THRONE
- 1 chair
- large fabric pieces
- sturdy tape
- junk jewelry
- safety pins

Drape the chairs with fabric. Tape securely on back and bottom of chairs. Pin jewelry along the top and sides of the chairs.

APPENDIX C: PROPS
PROPS LIST

Checkbooks & Other Banking Props (optional)
Drakesbill's Bank Deposit Money

APPENDIX D: COSTUMES
COSTUMES LIST

DRAKESBILL: plain, yellow clothes, duck-bill hat, feathered tail and web feet
BANK TELLER, BANK CUSTOMERS, AGENT: plain clothes
RENARD: plain, red or brown clothes with ears and tail
ÉCHELLE: plain, dark clothes with cardboard ladder attached
RIVIÈRE: plain, blue clothes with blue scarves or fabric pieces pinned on
LE NID DES GUÊPES: plain, dark clothes wrapped around with many ace bandages
GUÊPES: plain, dark clothes with antennae, stingers, and wings
LE ROI: royal clothes with crown
SERVANTS: plain clothes, may have aprons, work hats, and so on
GUARDS: plain clothes with matching tunics, hats, swords, and so forth
FLAMES: plain, fire-colored clothes with fire-colored scarves or fabric pieces pinned on

HOW TO MAKE THE COSTUMES

DUCK BILL
- plain, yellow baseball hat
- light cardboard
- pencil
- orange construction paper
- scissors
- glue

Draw a large duck bill on paper and cut out. Glue bill to a piece of cardboard and cut cardboard to same size. Glue bill to the visor of the baseball hat. (If there is any writing on the hat, cover with yellow paper or paint.)

DUCK TAIL
- feathers (real or make out of paper)
- long, elastic strip
- scissors
- masking tape
- string

Measure and tie the elastic to fit around the actor's waist. Cut string into several pieces, each approximately 30 cm long. Attach feathers all along the string pieces by wrapping a piece of tape around each feather stem and then wrapping it securely around the string. Tie the string pieces to the elastic waistband.

WEBBED FEET
- yellow construction paper or light cardboard
- pencil
- scissors
- tape

Draw 2 duck feet on paper or cardboard, large enough to cover the actor's shoes, and cut out. Tape to the top of the shoes. Another option is yellow swim fins, but these greatly limit the actor's mobility.

FOX EARS
- red or brown construction paper
- scissors
- light cardboard, glue (optional)
- markers, crayons, paint with brushes, (optional)
- fake fur, glue (optional)
- pencil
- stapler

Draw and cut out shape of fox ears with pencil on appropriate color of paper.
Cut a long strip of the same color, approximately 4 cm wide and long enough to go around the actor's head with a 2-3 centimeters of overlap. Staple ears to strip, and staple strips to fit snugly around the actor's head. You may want to reinforce ears and strips with a cardboard backing. Decorate as needed with markers, crayons, paint, or bits of fake fur.

FOX TAIL
- 3 long strips of light, red or brown fabric, approximately 1 meter long
- scissors
- long, elastic strip or safety pins

Braid together and tie in a knot at either end. Tail is either pinned to back of actor's pants or tied to an elastic strip that is measured and tied to fit around actor's waist. The best place to pin the tail to pants is through belt loops. If you pin it directly to pants or shirt, it can rip the fabric if someone steps on the tail.

LADDER

- large pieces of sturdy, brown cardboard
- scissors
- yardstick or meter stick
- pencil

Using yardstick or meter stick, measure, draw, and cut out a ladder, approximately the same length as the actor and with enough space between two of the rungs for the actor's head to fit through. Actor holds the ladder in front of herself, placing her head in between the rungs.

WASP ANTENNAE & STINGERS

- colored pipe cleaners
- elastic strips
- plastic headbands

Measure and tie elastic strips to fit around actors' waists. Twist and shape pipe cleaners to create antennae and stingers. (Twisting together two or more colors creates a nice effect.) Attach pipe cleaners to the elastic strips for the stingers and the headbands for the antennae.

A NOTE ABOUT WASP WINGS:

Wings are not easy to make and require a lot of time. Wings can be purchased at costume supply stores. To make: Bend and shape coat hangers to make the wing frame, cover them with gauzy material which can be sewn or glued around the edges, and attach them to some sort of harness made of elastic or ribbons which can be tied around the actors' chests.

CROWN

- shiny, gold paper or cardboard
- fake jewels (try a craft supply store)
- glitter (optional)
- scissors
- glue

Draw the crown shape, flat, on the gold paper or cardboard. If using paper, measure and cut a piece of light cardboard to reinforce it and glue it on the back. Glue jewels and glitter to the crown and allow time to dry. Cut an extra strip of cardboard, if needed, and staple to the side of the crown so that it can go all the way around the actor's head, measured and stapled to fit.

SWORDS

- big Styrofoam or heavy cardboard pieces
- cutting tool
- duct tape

Draw sword shape on Styrofoam or cardboard and cut out. Completely cover with duct tape. If using cardboard, make sure it's very thick as lightweight cardboard will bend too easily during rehearsals.

SOUND:
Magic of the creatures becoming very small and going into Drakesbill's
mouth: percussion or other instruments

MUSIC:
Song: *"L'Autre Jour en Voulant Danser"* (included) or other French folksong
(optional)
Underneath Drakesbill's repeating "Quack, quack, quack" chant: percussion
or other instruments (optional)

L'AUTRE JOUR EN VOULANT DANSER
("The Other Day , While I Was Dancing")

THE FIREBIRD, THE HORSE OF POWER, AND CZAREVNA VASILISA
(Russia)

Here's a classic, Russian tale, another version of which is familiar to many as the ballet "The Firebird." Look for another tale about Vasilisa in Volume Two of this series, *Vasilisa Prekrasnaia* ("Vasilisa the Beautiful"), in which she meets up with the archetypal dark witch, Baba Yaga. Like all good, Russian stories, this one has many layers of deep meaning. The hero, the Archer, is on a journey to learn the meaning of fear. He is wise enough to follow the advice of his inner, nonrational instinct, represented by the Horse of Power, and this saves him from death at the hands of the Czar, who represents oppressive, "power-over" authority and greed. In the end, the Archer bravely (or stupidly?) faces his fear of death by rushing into the cauldron of boiling water and by this act of accepting fear and death, he is saved by his "feminine," magical self, represented by Vasilisa.

Even if you don't agree with my interpretation of this tale or don't care to analyze the story, you'll find this play is full of fun action and magic, with enough parts for lots of kids. This is one of the most complicated play productions in this volume because of the length and because it has no Narrator to guide the actors. The actors who play the lead characters – the Archer, the Horse, the Czar, and Vasilisa – need to be very capable and able to learn a lot of lines. The other characters can be played by several other actors who can work in groups and who have less to learn and memorize. The lines of the Servants can be parceled out as needed – I've labeled them Servant #1, #2, and so on for each scene for simplicity's sake.

The Russian language is written in the Cyrillic alphabet, the invention of which is attributed to St. Cyril (who died in 869), apostle of the Slavs. The Russian words in this script are written here with the Latin alphabet, spelled phonetically.

RUNNING TIME OF SHOW: *(approximate)*
25-30 minutes

REHEARSAL TIME NEEDED:
12-15 hours

OTHER PRODUCTION TIME NEEDED:
4-6 hours

CAST SIZE:
Minimum: 7 (Firebird, Vasilisa, and Stable Groom actors can play other characters; there can be a minimum of 2 Servants and 1 Sea Pony; Servant actors can also play Lobster Czar, Lobsters, and some of the Sea Ponies; and Courtiers can be eliminated.)
Maximum: 25-30 (There can be numerous Servants, Courtiers, Lobsters and Sea Ponies.)

GENDER OF CHARACTERS:
In the traditional story, the Archer and the Czar are male and Vasilisa is female but their genders could possibly be reversed for this play. All other characters can be played as either female or male.

CHARACTERS:
STABLE GROOM
HORSE OF POWER – a magical steed belonging to the Archer
ARCHER – a young man in service to the Tsar
CZAR – king of Russia
FIREBIRD – a beautiful, huge, golden bird, rarely seen
CZAREVNA VASILISA – from the Land of Never
SERVANTS
LOBSTER CZAR
GIANT LOBSTERS
SEA PONIES – attendants of Princess Vasilisa
COURTIERS (optional)

SCENE 1

(Setting: Russia, long ago. A forest and nearby, the palace of the CZAR. Upstage, on one side of stage, are 1-3 sturdy tables with blue fabric hanging down the sides. Under the tables is the golden casket and backstage is VASILISA'S boat. Next to the tables are chairs, stepladders or other access to the tabletops. In front of the tables is a freestanding wall of a forest scene. This wall is placed such that in Scene 2 actors can stand on the tables and look over the forest wall as if they were in the treetops. Overhead a huge, spectacular Firebird feather is suspended so that it can be easily dropped onto the stage. There may be a backdrop on the upstage wall of a fiery sunset. On the other side of the stage is the CZAR'S palace including a throne and possibly an interior wall. Backstage is a second throne and a cauldron big enough for an actor to fit inside. Down center is the palace courtyard—no set needed. LIGHTS UP. STABLE GROOM enters the courtyard, leading HORSE.)

GROOM: *Dobre d'yen!* Good day!

(HORSE whinnies. ARCHER enters, with bow and arrows.)

GROOM: *(To HORSE:)* Here comes your master, the young Archer! *(To ARCHER:) Dobre d'yen!*
ARCHER: *Dobre d'yen!*

(HORSE whinnies. GROOM gives the reins to ARCHER who climbs on HORSE – HORSE actor can walk on two feet while ARCHER walks closely behind, holding the reins.)

ARCHER: *Dosvedanya!*
GROOM: *Dosvedanya!*

(HORSE whinnies and HORSE & ARCHER exit and travel toward the forest. GROOM exits. ARCHER stops in the forest, underneath the Firebird feather. SOUND: CHIMES as the feather falls to the ground.)

ARCHER: *(Astonished.)* The Firebird has come this way!

(He gets off HORSE and bends down to pick up the feather.)

HORSE: *(Sternly.) Nyet!* Leave the golden feather where it lies!
ARCHER: *(Straightening up.)* But the *Czar* will be so pleased!

(Again, he reaches for the feather.)

HORSE: *Nyet!* If you take it, you will know the meaning of fear!

(ARCHER pauses, debates, then picks up the feather.)

HORSE: You'll be sorry...

(ARCHER gets on HORSE again and they travel back to the palace. ARCHER leaves HORSE in the courtyard while he exits. SERVANT enters the palace.)

SERVANT: *(Loudly.)* His majesty, the *Czar* of Russia!

(CZAR, COURTIERS, & SERVANTS enter the palace. CZAR sits on the throne.)

SERVANT: *(Loudly.)* The *Czar's* young Archer!

(ARCHER enters with feather and bows before the CZAR.)

ARCHER: Your majesty, I've brought you a feather from the Firebird!

(ALL are astonished.)

CZAR: *Harashow!* Good! ...Now, bring me the Firebird!
ALL: *(Shocked.)* Impossible!
CZAR: Do as I say or your head shall no longer sit between your shoulders!

(ARCHER, miserable, bows and exits palace. CZAR, COURTIERS, & SERVANTS exit. ARCHER goes to the courtyard, weeping.)

HORSE: Master, why do you weep?
ARCHER: The *Czar* ordered me to bring him the Firebird! No one can do that!
HORSE: I told you you would learn the meaning of fear!

(ARCHER groans.)

HORSE: Tell the *Czar* to have a hundred sacks of maize scattered over an open field at midnight!
ARCHER: *Da!*

(ARCHER exits. LIGHTS down.)

SCENE 2

(Setting: An open field – center stage. SERVANTS enter with big sacks. LIGHTS are DIM to indicate night.)

SERVANT #1: Here's where we're supposed to spread the maize!

(SERVANTS pantomime spreading maize from the sacks.)

SERVANT #2: Do you think the Archer will really capture the Firebird?

SERVANT #3: Let's hide in the trees and watch!

(SERVANTS "climb" into the treetops by standing on the tables behind the forest scene wall. LIGHTS UP. ARCHER, with rope, & HORSE enter. ARCHER gets off HORSE and hides in the trees while HORSE stands nearby. SOUND EFFECTS: WIND and CHIMES. The actors in the treetops shake the forest set. FIREBIRD enters, stops, and eats the maize. SOUNDS STOP. HORSE comes close to her and suddenly steps on one of her wings, pinning her down. FIREBIRD screams with fright and ARCHER jumps out of tree and throws rope around her. ARCHER gets on HORSE and they lead FIREBIRD away and exit. SERVANTS, excited about what they've just seen, jump down out of trees and exit. CZAR, COURTIERS & SERVANTS, enter the palace and CZAR sits on the throne. One SERVANT stands by the entrance to the palace.)

SERVANT: *(Loudly.)* The *Czar's* young Archer and the Firebird!

(ARCHER & FIREBIRD enter. ALL are astonished.)

CZAR: *Harashow!* ...Now, if you can bring me the Firebird, surely you can bring me my bride! In the Land of Never, on the very edge of the world, lives the *Czarevna* Vasilisa! Bring her to me!

ALL: *(Shocked.)* Impossible!

CZAR: Do as I say or your head shall no longer sit between your shoulders!

(ARCHER, miserable, bows, and exits palace. CZAR, COURTIERS, SERVANTS, & FIREBIRD exit. ARCHER goes to the courtyard, weeping.)

HORSE: Master, why do you weep?

ARCHER: The *Czar* ordered me to go to the Land of Never and bring back the *Czarevna* Vasilisa! No one can do that!

HORSE: I told you you would learn the meaning of fear!

(ARCHER groans.)

HORSE: Go to the *Czar* and ask him for a silver tent with a golden roof and all kinds of food and drink!

ARCHER: *Da!*

(ARCHER & HORSE exit. LIGHTS DOWN. Change set: Remove the forest wall.)

SCENE 3

(Setting: The Land of Never – the tables upstage with blue fabric hanging down the sides are the deep blue sea. LIGHTS UP. ARCHER, HORSE & SERVANTS enter. The SERVANTS carry the silver tent with a golden roof – a light, freestanding wall, now folded up – plus 2 fancy cushions and food and drink props. SERVANTS are very tired.)

SERVANT #1: Are we there yet?!!

SERVANT #2: This silver tent gets heavier every day!

SERVANT #3: *(Pointing.)* Look! It's the deep blue sea where the red sun rises in flames!

SERVANT #4: We've come to the edge of the world!

(MUSIC: VASILISA enters in a silver boat with golden oars – this can be a decorated child's wagon or large cardboard box. She is attended by her SEA PONIES who pull her boat, paddle the oars, and dance around her.)

SERVANT #5: *(Pointing.)* Czarevna Vasilisa is coming in her silver boat with her Sea Ponies!

ARCHER: Get ready!

(SERVANTS quickly set up the silver tent, cushions, and food and drink props on the tabletops and then stand in attendance. ARCHER may put on a fancy shirt or vest. He sits in the tent while HORSE stands nearby. VASILISA & SEA PONIES come closer, frightened but fascinated by the silver tent. She gets out of the boat and approaches the tent, while SEA PONIES wait by the boat. MUSIC ends.)

ARCHER: *Dobre d'yen, Czarevna* Vasilisa! Come in!

(VASILISA hesitates and then comes and sits in the tent. SERVANT approaches with a wine bottle.)

SERVANT: *Veeno, Czarevna?* Wine?

VASILISA: *Da, pujhalsta.*

(SERVANT pours the wine – pantomime.)

VASILISA: *Spaseeba.*

(She drinks the wine and becomes sleepy.)

VASILISA: *(Yawns.)* It's only noon, yet I want to sleep....

(She yawns again and drops off to sleep.)

ARCHER: *Harashow!*

(He takes the sleeping VASILISA by the hand, leads her to his HORSE, puts her on the HORSE and gets on behind her. Meanwhile, the SERVANTS pick up the tent and props. SEA PONIES cry sadly as ARCHER, VASILISA, HORSE & SERVANTS exit. Then PONIES exit, with boat. LIGHTS DOWN.)

SCENE 4

(Setting: The CZAR'S palace, sometime later. CZAR & COURTIERS enter and CZAR sits on the throne. LIGHTS UP. One SERVANT enters and stands by the entrance to the palace.)

SERVANT: *(Loudly.)* The *Czar's* young Archer and the *Czarevna* Vasilisa!

(ARCHER, VASILISA & SERVANTS enter. VASILISA is sleepwalking. ALL are astonished.)

CZAR: *Harashow!* Ring the bells for our wedding!

(SOUND: BELLS. The sound wakes up VASILISA. She looks around, disoriented and confused. BELLS STOP.)

VASILISA: Why are bells ringing? Where are my silver boat and my Sea Ponies?

CZAR: The deep blue sea is far away. The bells are ringing for our wedding!

VASILISA: *(Horrified.)* OUR WEDDING?!!

(She looks at the CZAR and then at the ARCHER. She thinks for a moment and comes up with an idea.)

VASILISA: *(To CZAR:)* In the middle of the deep blue sea lies a big stone and under that stone is my wedding dress in a golden casket. If I can't wear that dress I will marry no one at all!

CZAR: *(To ARCHER:)* Go back to the Land of Never and bring back the dress!

ALL: *(Shocked.)* Impossible!

CZAR: Do as I say or your head shall no longer sit between your shoulders!

(ARCHER, miserable, bows and exits the palace.)

SERVANT: *(To VASILISA:)* Come, *Czarevna,* we'll take you to your chambers.

VASILISA: *Spaseeba.*

(VASILISA & SERVANTS begin to exit. She ignores the CZAR which upsets him.)

CZAR: *(Pleading.)* Czarevna Vasilisa! I'm sure you'll learn to love me!

VASILISA: Fat chance!

(VASILISA & SERVANTS exit. The CZAR & COURTIERS exit. ARCHER & HORSE enter courtyard.)

HORSE: Master, why do you weep?

ARCHER: The *Czar* ordered me to bring back the *Czarevna's* wedding dress from the bottom of the deep blue sea! No one can do that!

HORSE: I told you you would learn the meaning of fear!

ARCHER: Don't remind me!

HORSE: Follow me!

ARCHER: *Da!*

(They exit. LIGHTS DOWN.)

SCENE 5

(Setting: The Land of Never, sometime later. LIGHTS UP. ARCHER & HORSE enter. LOBSTER CZAR enters, moving slowly toward the deep blue sea.)

LOBSTER CZAR: *(Singing tunelessly:)*
I am the Lobster *Czar,*
the Giant Lobsters' Emperor!
I am the...

(Suddenly, HORSE steps on LOBSTER CZAR'S tail, pinning him down. LOBSTER CZAR screams and struggles to escape.)

LOBSTER CZAR: You will be the death of me! Let me live and I will do whatever you ask!

HORSE: *Harashow!*

(She takes her foot off LOBSTER CZAR'S tail.)

HORSE: In the middle of the deep blue sea lies a great stone and under that stone is the wedding dress of *Czarevna* Vasilisa in a golden casket. Bring it here!

LOBSTER CZAR: *Da! (Calls out.)* LOBSTERS! LOBSTERS! LOBSTERS!

(LOBSTERS enter from beneath the sea – from under the blue fabric – and gather around the LOBSTER CZAR.)

LOBSTER CZAR: Go get *Czarevna* Vasilisa's wedding dress!

LOBSTERS: *Da!*

(They go beneath the sea and return with a golden casket.)

ARCHER & HORSE: *Harashow!*

(ARCHER takes the casket and gets on HORSE.)

ARCHER & HORSE: *Dosvedanya!*
LOBSTER CZAR & LOBSTERS: *Dosvedanya!*

(ARCHER & HORSE exit. LOBSTER CZAR & LOBSTERS exit. LIGHTS DOWN. Add a second throne to the palace.)

SCENE 6

(Setting: The CZAR'S palace, sometime later. CZAR, VASILISA, COURTIERS & SERVANTS enter and CZAR & VASILISA sit on thrones. One SERVANT stands by the entrance to the palace. LIGHTS UP.)

SERVANT: *(Loudly.)* The *Czar's* young Archer and the golden casket!

(ARCHER enters with casket. COURTIERS & SERVANTS are astonished.)

CZAR: *Harashow!*

(ARCHER places the casket on the floor in front of VASILISA. She opens it and pulls out a beautiful dress.)

CZAR: Ring the bells for our wedding!

(SOUND: BELLS. VASILISA gives the CZAR a dirty look and exits to put on the dress. BELLS STOP. CZAR, ARCHERS & COURTIERS exit. SERVANTS put up some wedding decorations.)

SERVANT #1: *(To other SERVANTS:)* I think *Czarevna* Vasilisa and the young Archer are in love!
SERVANT #2: But she has to marry that ugly *Czar!*
SERVANT #3: Shhh!! He's coming!

(CZAR, ARCHER & COURTIERS enter. CZAR may have on a wedding shirt or vest. One SERVANT stands by entrance to the palace.)

SERVANT: *Czarevna* Vasilisa, from the Land of Never!

(VASILISA enters in wedding dress.)

CZAR: *Czarevna Vasilisa!* My bride!
VASILISA: *Nyet!* I will marry no one until the man who brought me here has been put in boiling water!

(ALL are astonished.)

CZAR: *Harashow!* Servants! Throw the young Archer in a pot of boiling water!

(SERVANTS bring out a cauldron and pantomime making a fire underneath it.)

ARCHER: *(Miserable, to CZAR:)* Before I die, may I see my horse, *pujhalsta?*
CZAR: *Nyet!*
VASILISA: Idiot! Let him see his horse!
CZAR: *(Cowed by her.) Da...*But hurry!

(ARCHER exits and goes to courtyard as HORSE enters. He throws his arms around his HORSE, crying.)

HORSE: Master, why do you weep?
ARCHER: The *Czar* has ordered me to be boiled to death! *Dosvedanya!*
HORSE: I suppose by now you've learned the meaning of fear ...
ARCHER: Okay, okay!
HORSE: When the water is boiling, run and leap in it!
ARCHER: *(Resigned.) Da.*

(ARCHER goes back to the palace.)

VASILISA: *(To SERVANTS:)* Are you sure the water is boiling?
SERVANTS: *Da!*
VASILISA: Let me see for myself.

(She goes over to cauldron and secretly waves her hand over it, sprinkling magic powder inside.)

VASILISA: It's ready!
CZAR: Servants! Throw him in!

(SERVANTS grab ARCHER but he throws them off and then takes a running leap into the cauldron. He rises to the surface and sinks down again two times. Then he rises up wearing a beautiful, glittering crown. ALL are astonished.)

SERVANT #1: He is beautiful! *Prekrasnaia!*
CZAR: I, too, will become *prekrasnaia!*

(CZAR takes a running leap into the cauldron and cries out in agony as he is boiled to death. Silence. SERVANTS look into cauldron.)

SERVANTS: The *Czar* is dead!

(ALL cheer.)

SERVANT #2: *(To ARCHER:)* Will you be our new *czar?*

ARCHER: *Da,* but only if *Czarevna* Vasilisa will marry me and rule by my side!

VASILISA: Why do you think I planned this whole thing? Of course I'll marry you!

(ALL cheer. May do song/dance, such as "Ladushki" or other Russian folksong.)

ALL: *Conyetz!* The end!

(LIGHTS DOWN.)

APPENDIX A: VOCABULARY LIST OF
FOREIGN LANGUAGE

RUSSIAN (latin alphabet)	ENGLISH	PRONUNCIATION
conyetz	the end	cone-yetz'
czar	king, emperor	tzar
da	yes	dah
dobre d'yen	good day	doh'-bree d'yen'
dosvedanya	good-bye, until later	doe-s'vee-don'-yah
harashow	good	ha'-ra-show
ladushki (song, included)	my little sweethearts (old Russian)	la'-doosh-key
nyet	no	n'yet
pujhalsta	please	puh-jhall'-eh'stuh
prekrasnaia	beautiful	preh-krah'-snay-ah
czarevna	princess, daughter of the czar	tsar-ehv'-nah
spaseeba	thank you	spah-see'-buh
veeno	wine	vee'-no

SETS LIST

FOREST:
> freestanding wall of forest scene
> tables or chairs behind the forest wall (see Land of Never)

PALACE:
> 2 thrones
> interior wall, freestanding or other (optional)

LAND OF NEVER:
> 1-3 sturdy tables
> chairs, stepladders, or other access to tabletops
> large, blue fabric pieces, taped on
> fiery sunrise backdrop (optional)

HOW TO MAKE THE SETS

FREESTANDING WALL (for forest scene, palace interior, and silver tent)
- very large cardboard box
- cardboard cutting knife
- scissors
- heavy butcher paper
- tape or glue
- markers, crayons or paint with brushes
- colored paper or fabric (optional)

Cut box to create a freestanding wall with accordion folds. Cut a piece of butcher paper to size of the wall. Tape or glue paper to the wall (if cardboard is plain white, you can eliminate this step). Draw picture of the set on the wall with markers, crayons, or paint. Colored paper or fabric can also be used to decorate the wall, using glue or tape. Silver tent can be covered with aluminum foil or silver paint, with top, the "roof," being covered with gold paper or paint.

THRONES
- 2 chairs
- large fabric pieces
- sturdy tape
- junk jewelry
- safety pins

Drape the chairs with fabric. Tape securely on back and bottom of chairs. Pin jewelry along the top and sides of the chairs.

LANDSCAPE BACKDROP
- heavy butcher paper
- markers, crayons or paint with brushes
- sturdy tape
- scissors

Cut butcher paper to fit across upstage wall. Draw scenes of a fiery sunrise with markers, crayons, or paint. Make sure the artists understand which end is up and that drawings must be large enough to be seen from the audience. Tape to wall.

APPENDIX C: PROPS

PROPS LIST

Firebird Feather
Large Sacks – one for each Servant
Rope
Silver Tent with Golden Roof
Food & Drink Props (optional)
Wine Bottle
Wine Glass (plastic)
2 Cushions
Silver Boat
Golden Oars
Golden Casket (decorated box, with lid)
Wedding Dress (see Costumes)
Large Cauldron (large, decorated box, no lid)
Crown (for Archer, see Costumes)

HOW TO MAKE THE PROPS

FIREBIRD FEATHER
- large piece of cardboard
- cutting tool
- gold, red, orange and/or yellow paper or paint with brush
- colored feathers (optional)
- scissors
- glue
- glitter (optional)
- string or fishing line

Draw a huge feather shape on the cardboard and cut out. Cover both sides with colored paper or paint. Draw smaller feathers on other paper, cut out, cut fringe around the edges, and glitter (or use real feathers). Glue the feathers onto the cardboard by the stems only, so that they create a 3-D effect. Attach string or fishing line to the center of the feather and throw the other end of the string over an overhead pipe, pulling to suspend it over the stage. If there's nothing overhead from which to suspend the feather, it can be tossed onstage from backstage.

SILVER TENT
(See How To Make Sets, freestanding walls)

SILVER BOAT
- child's wagon
- cardboard cutting tool
- silver paper or aluminum foil or silver paint with brushes
- scissors & glue
- large cardboard pieces
- sturdy tape
- silver glitter (optional)

Cut cardboard to represent the sides of the boat. Decorate with paper, foil, paint and/or glitter. Tape securely to sides of the wagon, making sure that the actor can still fit inside. Sea Ponies pull/push the wagon.

GOLDEN OARS
- 2 long poles
- cardboard cutting tool
- paint, glitter, as needed
- 2 pieces of thick cardboard
- tape

Draw a large circle on the cardboard, slightly oblong, and approx. 30 cm long. Draw a long tab at the bottom of it, for attaching the paddle to the pole. Cut out the paddle and tape it near the top of the pole. Paint and glitter as needed.

APPENDIX D: COSTUMES

COSTUMES LIST

HORSE: plain, horse-colored pants & shirt or leotard & tights, ears and tail, and "reins" (loose rope tied around chest or waist)

ARCHER: pants and shirt, possibly a tunic with belt, bow & arrows (optional – he never actually shoots); he also needs a spectacular crown for the end

CZAR: royal-looking clothes, may have crown

SERVANTS: plain, poor-looking clothes; may have tunics, aprons, and so on

FIREBIRD: gold, red, orange and/or yellow costume, with feathered headpiece and tail or feathered cape

VASILISA: beautiful dress or skirt and top, plus wedding dress which should be easy to put on quickly

LOBSTER CZAR & LOBSTERS: all red pants & shirt or leotard & tights, with headpieces; Czar may also have a crown

SEA PONIES: plain, colored pants & shirt or leotard & tights, with colored scarves and colored ears and tails

COURTIERS: fancy-looking clothes

HOW TO MAKE THE COSTUMES

HORSE EARS

- colored construction paper
- pencil
- scissors
- stapler
- light cardboard, glue (optional)
- markers, crayons, paint with brushes, (optional)
- fake fur, glue (optional)

Draw and cut out shape of ears with pencil on paper. Cut long strips of the same color, approximately 4 cm wide and long enough to go around the actor's heads with a 2-3 centimeters of overlap. Staple ears to strips, and staple strips to fit snugly around the actor's head. You may want to reinforce ears and strips with a cardboard backing. Decorate as needed with markers, crayons, or paint.

HORSE TAILS

- long strips, approx. 1 meter long, of colored chiffon or other light
- fabric
- scissors
- long, elastic strip or safety pins

Measure out three strips of fabric. Braid together and tie in a knot at either end. Tail is either pinned to back of actor's pants or tied to an elastic strip that is measured and tied to fit around actor's waist. The best place to pin the tail to pants is through belt loops. If you pin it directly to pants or shirt, it can rip the fabric if someone steps on the tail.

CROWNS

- shiny, gold paper or cardboard
- scissors
- glue
- fake jewels (try a craft supply store)
- gold and silver pipe cleaners (for Archer)
- glitter (optional)

Draw the crown shape, flat, on the gold paper or cardboard. If using paper, mea-

sure and cut a piece of light cardboard to reinforce it and glue it on the back. Glue jewels to the crown and allow time to dry. Cut a strip of the gold paper or cardboard 5 cm wide and staple to the crown, measuring the whole to fit around the actor's head. For the Archer's crown, gold and silver pipe cleaners can be added as rays of brilliance.

FIREBIRD HEAD & TAIL PIECES

- gold, red, orange and/or yellow paper, scissors

OR

- colored feathers
- tape
- 2 long, elastic strips
- fabric cape, stapler (optional

Measure and tie a piece of elastic to fit around the actor's head and another piece to fit around the actor's waist. Draw smaller feathers on paper, cut out, cut fringe around the edges, and glitter (or use real feathers). Tape the feathers to the elastic so that they hang down. A cape could also be fashioned out of a piece of fabric with feathers stapled on.

LOBSTER HEADPIECES

- pipe cleaners, any color
- plastic headbands

Twist and shape pipe cleaners to create antennae. (Twisting together two or more colors creates a nice effect.) Attach pipe cleaners to the headbands.

APPENDIX E: SOUND & MUSIC

SOUND:

Firebird feather falling and Firebird entrance: chimes or other, magical sound
Firebird entrance (wind): a flexible, plastic pipe that can be twirled, or create sound vocally
Wedding bells: hand bells or other bells

MUSIC:

Vasilisa's entrance music: any pretty music, played live or on tape
"Ladushki" (included) or other Russian folksong (optional)
Russian music to play during the scene changes, either played live or on tape or CD

LADUSHKI
("My Little Sweethearts")

Russian folk song

La - dush- ki, la -dush- ki, *(clap hands)*

la - dush- ki, la -dush - ki, *(clap hands)*

la - dush- ki, la -dush- ki, la - dush- ki, la -dush- ki,

la - dush- ki, la -dush- ki, la -dush- ki la - don,

la - dush - ki, la - dush - ki.

THE GREAT BEAR
(China)

There are many myths from around the world about the stars and their constellations. This play is based on a myth about how the constellation *Ursa Major* was created. The story comes from the Ordos people, a Mongolion people who live in the Ordos Desert region between the Yellow River and the Great Wall of China.

Ursa Major ("Greater Bear," also called Great Bear) is the most conspicuous constellation in the northern sky. It is situated near the north pole of the heavens and contains the stars which form the Big Dipper, two of which are in a line that points to the North Star. *Ursa Minor* ("Lesser Bear," also called Little Bear) includes the stars which form the Little Dipper, with the North Star at the tip of the handle.

This play has a lot of physical action scenes which are really fun but require careful planning and control. A production of *The Great Bear* can be integrated with a unit on astronomy, mythology, or a comparison between *Ursa Major* stories.

RUNNING TIME OF THE SHOW: *(approximate)*
20 minutes
REHEARSAL TIME NEEDED:
8-10 hours
OTHER PRODUCTION TIME NEEDED:
2-3 hours
CAST SIZE:
Minimum: 12, plus Narrator (Khan, Khan's Son and Warriors can also play the Gazelles.)
Maximum: 20-25 (There can be numerous Gazelles and Warriors)
GENDER OF CHARACTERS:
All the major characters are traditionally portrayed as male but can be played as either male or female.

CHARACTERS:
NARRATOR
THE ADVENTURERS:
    1st HUNTER
    2nd HUNTER
    SKY SHOOTER
    GREAT LISTENER
    MOUNTAIN LIFTER
    SWIFT RUNNER
    SEA SWALLOWER
GAZELLES
KHAN SADZAGHAI
KHAN'S SON
KHAN'S WARRIORS:
    CHIEF ARCHER
    CHIEF WRESTLER
    OLD WOMAN RUNNER
    OTHER WARRIORS (optional)

SCENE 1

(Setting: The Ordos Desert region of China. Center stage is left open, around which are several mountains, represented by large, sturdy tables with cloth hanging down the sides, and slides, chairs or other access to tabletops. There are also a couple of mountains which MOUNTAIN LIFTER actor can move about, made of smaller tables or chairs, covered with a dark cloth. There are a few freestanding trees downstage on one side of the stage. There is a bird prop suspended from the ceiling by a string which can be easily released. If there is nothing overhead from which to hang the string, the bird can simply be tossed from backstage. On one side of the stage is a great sea, made of a long, blue cloth laid on the floor. LIGHTS UP.)

NARRATOR: Long ago, in the Ordos Desert region of the land we now call China, between the Yellow River, the *Hwang Ho*, and the Great Wall of China, two young adventurers went hunting.

(HUNTERS enter, possibly carrying bows and arrows.)

NARRATOR: They soon met a young man who carried a bow and arrows.

(SKY SHOOTER enters, gazing up at the sky.)

HUNTERS: What are you doing?
SKY SHOOTER: This morning I shot a bird flying in heaven and now I'm waiting for it to fall.

(SOUND: Slide whistle. Bird with arrow in it falls from the sky.)

HUNTERS: *(To each other:)* And we thought *we* were good hunters!
(To Sky Shooter:) Will you be our blood brother and travel with us?
SKY SHOOTER: Okay!

(They travel to the top of a mountain as GREAT LISTENER enters there and places her ear to the ground.)

NARRATOR: On top of the next mountain they saw a woman lying down with her ear to the ground.
HUNTERS & SKY SHOOTER: What are you doing?

GREAT LISTENER: I'm listening to the earth and sky. I can hear everything that people are saying in both worlds.

HUNTERS & SKY SHOOTER: *(To each other:)* And we thought <u>we</u> had good ears! *(To GREAT LISTENER:)* Will you be our blood sister and travel with us?

GREAT LISTENER: Okay!

(They continue to travel as MOUNTAIN LIFTER enters and moves around two mountains.)

NARRATOR: Soon they came to a man standing between two mountains which he kept moving about.

HUNTERS, SKY SHOOTER & GREAT LISTENER: What are you doing?

MOUNTAIN LIFTER: I'm just exercising, to cure the rheumatism in my arms.

HUNTERS, SKY SHOOTER & GREAT LISTENER: And we thought *we* were strong! *(To MOUNTAIN LIFTER:)* Will you be our blood brother and travel with us?

MOUNTAIN LIFTER: Okay!

(They continue to travel as SWIFT RUNNER and GAZELLES enter. SWIFT RUNNER chases the GAZELLES, captures them one by one and then lets them loose.)

NARRATOR: On an open plain they saw a woman chasing gazelles, capturing them one by one, then letting them loose.

HUNTERS, SKY SHOOTER, GREAT LISTENER & MOUNTAIN LIFTER: What are you doing?

SWIFT RUNNER: I'm just playing with these gazelles.

HUNTERS, SKY SHOOTER, GREAT LISTENER & MOUNTAIN LIFTER: And we thought *we* were fast! *(To SWIFT RUNNER:)* Will you be our blood sister and travel with us?

SWIFT RUNNER: Okay!

(They continue to travel.)

NARRATOR: As the Adventurers traveled they wondered what they should do to earn their living. They asked Great Listener to put her ear to the ground and find out what was happening on earth.

(GREAT LISTENER does so.)

GREAT LISTENER: Beyond the great sea a Khan named Sadzaghai is making plans to conquer our empire. Let's stop him!

ALL OTHERS: Great idea!

NARRATOR: They set off at once for the realm of the Khan Sadzaghai.

(They travel to the sea while SEA SWALLOWER enters there.)

NARRATOR: Soon they came to the great sea and asked the woman sitting there how they could cross the water.

SEA SWALLOWER: That's easy!

(SEA SWALLOWER "swallows" all the water – actor actually stuffs the blue cloth in her shirt while pretending to swallow it.)

SEA SWALLOWER: Now you can cross!

ALL OTHERS: And we thought *we* had big mouths! *(To SEA SWAL-LOWER:)* Will you be our blood sister and travel with us?

SEA SWALLOWER: Okay!

(They travel across the sea bed. When they get to the other side, SEA SWALLOWER "spits" out the water. They continue to travel. KHAN'S SON enters.)

NARRATOR: After awhile they met a handsome young man carrying a bow and arrow. They told him they were going to the city of Khan Sadzaghai.

KHAN'S SON: Why are you going there?

ALL OTHERS: We would like to serve the Khan.

KHAN'S SON: Then let's go to his palace. I am the Khan's son!

(ALL exit. LIGHTS DOWN. Set up KHAN'S palace set.)

SCENE 2

(Setting: The Khan's palace. The tables or other furniture that have been used as the mountains set can be used now to create levels of the palace set. On one side of the stage is the palace interior which may include an interior wall. There is a banquet table and possibly a few chairs backstage. On the other side of the stage is the gate to the palace and outside the gate is an area where the Adventurers can lay down to sleep, possibly on the tabletop. There is space down center for the fol-

lowing contest, while trees remain in place. LIGHTS UP. The
KHAN'S SON & ADVENTURERS enter near the palace gate.)

NARRATOR: The Khan's son escorted them to a magnificent city. He
left them at the gate to the palace while he went to tell his father of
their arrival.

(KHAN'S SON goes into the palace as KHAN enters there.)

KHAN'S SON: Father, today I met seven young Adventurers who
want to serve you.

KHAN: Are they worthy? Tomorrow we'll test them and see! Here's my
plan.

*(KHAN & KHAN'S SON pantomime talking together. Meanwhile,
GREAT LISTENER puts her ear to the ground.)*

GREAT LISTENER: *(To the others:)* They say that tomorrow we'll
have an archery contest.

SKY SHOOTER: Don't worry, I'll take care of it!

(LIGHTS DOWN.)

SCENE 3

(Setting: The same, the next morning. LIGHTS UP.)

NARRATOR: The next day the Adventurers met with the Khan, his
Chief Archer, and some of his best warriors.

*(CHIEF ARCHER & OTHER WARRIORS enter. ALL meet center
stage.)*

SKY SHOOTER: *(To CHIEF ARCHER:)* You can go first.

*(SOUND: GONG or other signal for the beginning of the contest.
CHIEF ARCHER shoots – either pantomime or have enough room to
shoot toy arrows across the stage. SKY SHOOTER shoots and the
arrow goes farther. The ADVENTURERS cheer while KHAN & CO.
are angry.)*

NARRATOR: Sky Shooter easily defeated the Khan's Chief Archer and
the Khan was outraged. He gathered his warriors together to plan
the next contest.

(KHAN, KHAN'S SON & WARRIORS huddle together and pantomime talking while in another area of the stage the ADVENTURERS gather around GREAT LISTENER while she puts her ear to the ground.)

GREAT LISTENER: *(To the Adventurers:)* They say that tomorrow we'll have a wrestling match.

MOUNTAIN LIFTER: Don't worry, I'll take care of it!

(ADVENTURERS go to the area by the palace gate, lay down and go to sleep.)

NARRATOR: The Adventurers found a place to sleep outside the palace gate. Meanwhile, the Khan and his warriors went out into a field where there were trees growing at one end. They pulled some of the trees out by their roots and then stuck them in the ground at the other end.

(WARRIORS pick up some of the trees and place them on the other side of the stage, downstage. LIGHTS DOWN.)

SCENE 4

(Setting: The same, the next morning. LIGHTS UP.)

NARRATOR: The next morning, they all gathered on the field.

(The ADVENTURERS wake up and go to center stage where they meet the others.)

NARRATOR: The Khan explained the rules of the wrestling contest.

KHAN: Our Chief Wrestler will start at this end *(Points to end with the uprooted trees.)* and your wrestler will start at the other end. *(Points to other trees.)* They must pull out the trees as they move toward each other.

(CHIEF WRESTLER goes to side with uprooted trees, MOUNTAIN LIFTER goes to the other side. SOUND: GONG or other signal is sounded to begin the contest. The wrestlers pull up the trees and fling them aside as they come toward each other. CHIEF WRESTLER has trouble lifting trees while MOUNTAIN LIFTER lifts trees fast and easily. They meet in the center and wrestle. MOUNTAIN LIFTER

wins easily. The ADVENTURERS cheer while KHAN & CO. are angry.)

NARRATOR: Mountain Wrestler easily won, flinging aside the rooted trees far faster than the Khan's Chief Wrestler pulled up the rootless ones and swiftly pinning him in the match. The Khan was terribly angry – being beaten once was bad enough, but *twice* was intolerable. He and his warriors huddled together to choose a contest that would surely destroy these seven strangers.

(KHAN, KHAN'S SON & WARRIORS huddle together and pantomime talking together while in another area of the stage GREAT LISTENER puts her ear to the ground.)

GREAT LISTENER: *(To the others:)* They say that tomorrow we'll have a foot race.

SWIFT RUNNER: Don't worry, I'll take care of it!

(LIGHTS DOWN.)

SCENE 5

(Setting: The same, the next morning. LIGHTS UP.)

NARRATOR: The next morning, Swift Runner met her opponent: an old woman with very long legs who had never been beaten at racing.

(SWIFT RUNNER goes to starting point for race. OLD WOMAN RUNNER enters and stands next to her.)

NARRATOR: The Khan gave the signal to begin the race around two mountains.

(KHAN gives some sort of signal and SWIFT RUNNER & OLD WOMAN RUNNER take off, racing around the stage and audience. 2 actors hold up a finish line tape. Eventually the OLD WOMAN faints and falls and SWIFT RUNNER wins the race. The ADVENTURERS cheer while KHAN & CO. are angry.)

NARRATOR: By now, the Khan had had it with these Adventurers. Some of his most bloodthirsty warriors had ideas about how to destroy them once and for all.

(KHAN, KHAN'S SON & WARRIORS gather together while in another area of the stage, GREAT LISTENER puts her ear to the ground.)

WARRIOR #1: Let's invite them to a banquet in the iron house! Then we'll heap coal around the house...

WARRIOR #2: *(Getting the idea.)* And then we'll set fire to the coal!

WARRIOR #3: And burn them to death!

ALL: Ha, ha, ha! Let's do it!

GREAT LISTENER: *(To the others:)* They say that tomorrow they'll burn us to death in an iron house.

SEA SWALLOWER: Don't worry, I'll take care of it!

(SEA SWALLOWER goes to the sea, "swallows" it and comes back to where the ADVENTURERS are. KHAN & CO. bring a banquet table and possibly a few chairs into the palace. There may be a few food and beverage props on the table.)

SCENE 6

(Setting: The same.)

NARRATOR: The Khan sent a messenger to the Adventurers.

(WARRIOR goes to the ADVENTURERS.)

WARRIOR: The great Khan Sadzaghai is so impressed with your great skills that he would like to invite you to a royal banquet!

ADVENTURERS: We'd be honored!

(They give each other sly smiles and follow the WARRIOR to the banquet room where they sit or stand at the table. KHAN & CO. spread coals around the room and then pantomime lighting them. The Adventurers pantomime getting very hot and uncomfortable.)

ALL: It sure is getting HOT in here!!

SEA SWALLOWER: Don't worry – I told you I'd take care of it!

(SEA SWALLOWER "spits" out the sea and quenches the fire – actors spread the cloth all around the room. The ADVENTURERS sigh with relief.)

KHAN & CO.: *(Vexed.)* AAARRGGHH!!!

(They exit, yelling and screaming.)

MOUNTAIN LIFTER: Well, now that we've destroyed the Khan, what shall we do next?

SWIFT RUNNER: Let's go home!

(The ADVENTURERS move into position to form the constellation on stage. Each holds up a large star.)

NARRATOR: They returned to the land from which they came. Then they ascended into heaven and became the seven stars of the constellation *Ursa Major,* the Great Bear. There they live very happily and peacefully.

ALL: The end!

(LIGHTS DOWN.)

APPENDIX B: SETS

SETS LIST

MOUNTAINS:
- 1 or more sturdy tables
- slides, chairs or other access to tabletops
- large, plain dark fabric pieces to hang down the sides (taped on)

PALACE:
- banquet table
- chairs (optional)
- freestanding wall or other interior backdrop (optional)

TREES:
- 4 or more freestanding, cardboard tree sets

HOW TO MAKE THE SETS

TREES
- large pieces of sturdy cardboard
- cutting tool
- colored construction paper, scissors, glue OR paint, brushes
- stands, such as music stands or microphone stands, or chairs (optional)

Trees can either be made in a "v" or "u" shape in order to stand by themselves, or can be two-dimensional and secured to some sort of stand or a chair. Draw tree shape on cardboard and cut out. Decorate with either construction paper or paint. Tape to stand if needed.

FREESTANDING WALL (for palace interior)
- very large, cardboard box
- cardboard cutting knife
- scissors
- heavy butcher paper
- tape or glue
- markers, crayons or paint with brushes
- colored paper or fabric (optional)

Cut box to create a freestanding wall with accordion folds. Cut a piece of butcher paper to size of the wall. Tape or glue paper to the wall (if cardboard is plain

white, you can eliminate this step). Draw picture of the set on the wall with mark-
ers, crayons, or paint. Colored paper or fabric can also be used to decorate the wall,
using glue or tape.

APPENDIX C: PROPS

PROPS LIST

Bow & Arrows – 2 or more sets (for Sky Shooter, Chief Archer and
  possibly 1st and 2nd Hunters and Other Warriors)
Bird with Arrow in it
Sea (long, blue cloth)
Finish Line Tape
Food & Beverage Props (optional)
Coal (wadded-up black construction paper)
Stars (cardboard and glitter – may be mounted on a stick)

APPENDIX D: COSTUMES

ALL ADVENTURERS, CHIEF ARCHER, CHIEF WRESTLER, OLD
  WOMAN RUNNER, AND OTHER WARRIORS: tunics with belts
  and pants
KHAN, KHAN'S SON: same as the above, but more rich-looking
GAZELLES: plain pants and shirts, may add tails

APPENDIX E: SOUND & MUSIC

SOUND:
  Bird falling from sky: slide whistle
  Signal for contests: gong or other signal

I DODICI MESI
"The Twelve Months"
(Italy)

Folktales have a way of traveling about, without regard to national boundaries. There are countless examples of stories that can be found, with local variations, all over the globe. Examining the cross-cultural-ism of folklore teaches students about what is common across the great diversity of the world's cultures.

I found one version of this story listed as a French tale and another version listed as Italian. However, the names Dobrunka and Katinka sound Slavic and this same story is also told in Russia about Marushka and her stepsister Holena. My Italian friend conjectures that the tale comes from the Northeastern corner of Italy, which borders on the Slavic country of Slovenia and where Slovene language and culture per-sist, despite being inside the border of Italy, and has traveled at least as far as France. Here, I've placed it in Italy with Italian language.

This is one of those ancient tales rich in archetypal imagery. Dobrunka represents the innocent child self who is abused and aban-doned and yet finds salvation in her pure alignment with the forces of nature. The Stepmother and Katinka represent the parts of the self who fear wholeness and thus try to inhibit the growth of the self. If read as an archetypal story, the Stepmother character is symbolic and is not a slander of actual stepmothers or women in general. The stepmother also represents the harsh reality of life when adopted children are resented as competitors for scarce resources such as property.

Producing this play can potentially be cathartic for young actors who relate to the feelings and experience of being abused or aban-doned, feelings most people have at some time or another. It can, how-ever, prove to be too close for comfort if any of the actors has or is cur-rently experiencing real abuse, or has a troublesome relationship with a parent. The line about "being beaten to a jelly" can be altered to a milder admonishment if needed.

There is a song/dance included with this script (a Jamaican song with Italian lyrics for a Slavic folktale—now that's multicultural!)

RUNNING TIME OF SHOW: *(approximate)*
    20-25 minutes
REHEARSAL TIME NEEDED:
    8-10 hours
OTHER PRODUCTION TIME NEEDED:
    3-4 hours
CAST SIZE:
    Minimum: 7, plus Narrator
    Maximum: 15
GENDER OF CHARACTERS:
    The Heroine (Dobrunka) and the Wicked Stepsister (Katinka) and Step-
mother are traditionally portrayed as females but it's possible to play them as
males, especially if you want to challenge the archetypal roles. The months can
be played as either male or female.

CHARACTERS:
    NARRATOR
    DOBRUNKA – a young girl
    KATINKA – Dobrunka's stepsister
    STEPMOTHER
    I DODICI MESI (The 12 Months):
        GENNAIO – January
        FEBBRAIO – February
        MARZO – March
        APRILE – April
        MAGGIO – May
        GIUGNO – June
        LUGLIO – July
        AGOSTO – August
        SETTEMBRE – September
        OTTOBRE – October
        NOVEMBRE – November
        DICEMBRE – December

SCENE 1

(Setting: One area of the stage is the cottage where DOBRUNKA, STEPMOTHER & KATINKA live. In the house are two chairs and there may be either a freestanding wall or backdrop of the house interior. The front door of the house can either be indicated by a set or pantomimed. In another area of the stage is the forested mountain, created by one or more large, sturdy tables, strong enough to support the actors, with slides or other access to the tabletops. On the tabletops the forest is indicated by either a freestanding wall or other backdrop of a winter scene and there is a fire pit down center. A freestanding wall with spring and summer backdrops and a tree set are backstage. There needs to be some source of light directed at the forest scene, such as from a lamp located on one side or from behind the audience. LIGHTS UP.)

NARRATOR: There was once a widow with two children: her daughter, Katinka, and her stepdaughter, Dobrunka.

(STEPMOTHER, KATINKA & DOBRUNKA enter. DOBRUNKA carries a broom. STEPMOTHER & KATINKA sit down.)

STEPMOTHER: Dobrunka!! Sweep the house, cook dinner, wash the clothes, cut the grass, and milk the cow!
DOBRUNKA: *Sì.*

(She sweeps.)

KATINKA: *(Coughs a little.)* Mama, Dobrunka is kicking up too much dust!
STEPMOTHER: Dobrunka, you are wicked for making your sister cough! Poor Katinka!

(KATINKA coughs and sticks her tongue out at DOBRUNKA.)

DOBRUNKA: I'll go cook dinner, instead.

(She exits.)

STEPMOTHER: *(To herself:)* That hateful Dobrunka grows more beautiful everyday just to spite me! Suitors will soon appear and will refuse Katinka when they see her stepsister! I must get rid of her!
KATINKA: Mama, I have a fancy for some *violette,* some violets!

STEPMOTHER: Dobrunka!! Come here!

(DOBRUNKA enters.)

DOBRUNKA: *Sì?*

STEPMOTHER: Go to the forest and bring back some *violette* for your sister!

DOBRUNKA: But it's *gennaio!* There are no *violette* under the snow!

KATINKA: Hold your tongue, stupid lass! If you don't get me some *violette* we will beat you to a jelly!

(They grab DOBRUNKA and throw her out the door and lock it behind her.)

STEPMOTHER & KATINKA: *Arrivederci!*

(They laugh wickedly, then exit. DOBRUNKA, crying, walks toward the forest.)

NARRATOR: The poor girl went to the forest, weeping bitterly. Everything was covered with snow and there was not even a footpath. By nightfall, she had lost her way and she wandered about, nearly freezing to death.

(LIGHTS DOWN)

All at once she saw a light in the distance, up on *la montagna*, the mountain.

(FOREST LIGHT ON.)

She went on toward the light on *la montagna* and as she got closer she began to hear music.

(MUSIC BEGINS: "I Dodici Mesi". MONTHS enter, singing and dancing, while DOBRUNKA approaches, watching. GENNAIO has a large staff. MONTHS suddenly see DOBRUNKA. MUSIC STOPS abruptly.)

JANUARY: Why have you come here, *fanciulla mia?*

DOBRUNKA: I am looking for some *violette!*

ANOTHER MONTH: But this is not the season for *violette!*

DOBRUNKA: I know, but if I don't bring back some *violette,* my stepmother and stepsister will beat me to a jelly!

JANUARY: *Sorella Marzo,* Sister March, this is your business.

(GENNAIO hands his staff to MARZO who stirs the fire with it. SOUND & LIGHT EFFECTS while a freestanding wall of a spring landscape is brought out and placed in front of the winter backdrop. Several violets are spread out in front of the backdrop.)

MARZO: Hurry, my child, and pick your *violette! Avanti, fanciulla mia!*
DOBRUNKA: *Grazie!*

(DOBRUNKA quickly gathers a bouquet and hurries toward home. FOREST LIGHT OFF. Remove spring backdrop. MONTHS exit. LIGHTS UP. STEPMOTHER & KATINKA enter the house as DOBRUNKA rushes up to them. She gives KATINKA the bouquet.)

STEPMOTHER & KATINKA: Where did you get these *violette??!!*
DOBRUNKA: Up on *la montagna!*

(STEPMOTHER & KATINKA try to hide their shock by sniffing disdainfully and turning away from DOBRUNKA, who exits.)

NARRATOR: Katinka didn't even thank her sister for *le violette.*

(LIGHTS DOWN – optional)

SCENE 2

(Setting: The same. LIGHTS UP.)

NARRATOR: The next morning the wicked Katinka wanted something else.
KATINKA: Mama, I have a fancy for some *fragole,* some strawberries!
STEPMOTHER: Dobrunka!!

(DOBRUNKA enters.)

DOBRUNKA: *Sì?*
STEPMOTHER: Go to the forest and bring back some *fragole* for your sister!
DOBRUNKA: But it's *gennaio!* There are no *fragole* under the snow!
KATINKA: Hold your tongue, stupid lass! If you don't get me some *fragole* we will beat you to a jelly!

(They grab DOBRUNKA and throw her out the door and lock it behind her.)

STEPMOTHER & KATINKA: *Arrivederci!*

(They laugh wickedly, then exit. DOBRUNKA, crying, walks toward the forest. LIGHTS DOWN. FOREST LIGHT ON. MUSIC BEGINS: "I Dodici Mesi." MONTHS enter, singing and dancing, while DOBRUNKA approaches, watching. MONTHS suddenly see DOBRUNKA. MUSIC STOPS abruptly.)

GENNAIO: Why have you come here, *fanciulla mia?*

DOBRUNKA: I am looking for some *fragole!*

ANOTHER MONTH: But this is not the season for *fragole!*

DOBRUNKA: I know, but if I don't bring back some *fragole* my stepmother and stepsister will beat me to a jelly!

GENNAIO: *Fratello Giugno,* Brother June, this is your business.

(GENNAIO gives his staff to GIUGNO who stirs the fire with it. SOUND & LIGHT EFFECTS while a freestanding wall of a summer backdrop is brought out and placed in front of the winter backdrop. A green cloth is laid on the floor on which are placed several strawberries. Someone gives DOBRUNKA a basket.)

GIUGNO: Hurry, my child, and gather your *fragole! Avanti, fanciulla mia!*

DOBRUNKA: *Grazie!*

(DOBRUNKA quickly picks the strawberries and puts them in the basket, then hurries toward home. FOREST LIGHT OFF. Remove summer backdrop and green cloth. MONTHS exit. LIGHTS UP. STEPMOTHER & KATINKA enter the house as DOBRUNKA rushes up to them. She gives KATINKA the basket of strawberries.)

STEPMOTHER & KATINKA: Where did you get these *fragole??!!*

DOBRUNKA: Up on *la montagna!*

(STEPMOTHER & KATINKA try to hide their shock by sniffing disdainfully and turning away from DOBRUNKA, who exits.)

NARRATOR: Katinka and her mother gobbled up *le fragole* without even thanking Dobrunka.

(LIGHTS DOWN – optional)

SCENE 3

(Setting: The same. LIGHTS UP.)

NARRATOR: On the third day, Katinka decided she wanted something else.

KATINKA: Mama, I have a fancy for some *mele*, some apples!

STEPMOTHER: Dobrunka!!

(DOBRUNKA enters.)

DOBRUNKA: *Sì?*

STEPMOTHER: Go to the forest and get your sister some *mele!*

DOBRUNKA: But its *gennaio!* There are no *mele* growing under the snow!

KATINKA: Hold your tongue, stupid lass! If you don't get me some *mele* we will beat you to a jelly!

(They grab DOBRUNKA and throw her out the door and lock it behind her.)

STEPMOTHER & KATINKA: *Arrivederci!*

(They laugh wickedly, then exit. DOBRUNKA, crying, walks toward the forest. LIGHTS DOWN. FOREST LIGHT ON. MUSIC BEGINS: "I Dodici Mesi." MONTHS enter, singing and dancing, while DOBRUNKA approaches, watching. MUSIC ENDS. They see DOBRUNKA.)

GENNAIO: Why have you come here, *fanciulla mia?*

DOBRUNKA: I am looking for some *mele!*

ANOTHER MONTH: But this is not the season for *mele!*

DOBRUNKA: I know, but if I don't bring back some *mele*, my stepmother and stepsister will beat me to a jelly!

GENNAIO: *Sorella Settembre*, this is your business.

(GENNAIO hands his staff to SETTEMBRE who stirs the fire with it. SOUND LIGHT EFFECTS while tree set is brought out and placed in front of the winter backdrop.)

SETTEMBRE: Hurry, my child, and shake the tree! *Avanti, fanciulla mia!*

(DOBRUNKA shakes the tree and an apple "falls" – a backstage person tosses the apple over the set. She shakes it again and another apple "falls." DOBRUNKA picks them up.)

DOBRUNKA: *Grazie!*

(DOBRUNKA hurries toward home. FOREST LIGHT OFF. Remove summer backdrop and green cloth. MONTHS exit. LIGHTS UP. STEPMOTHER & KATINKA enter the house as DOBRUNKA rushes up to them. She gives them the apples.)

STEPMOTHER & KATINKA: Where did you get these *mele??!!*
DOBRUNKA: Up on *la montagna!*
KATINKA: Why did you only bring two?!!
DOBRUNKA: I was only allowed to shake the tree twice!
STEPMOTHER: Get out of here!

> *(DOBRUNKA exits. STEPMOTHER & KATINKA gobble up the apples.)*

NARRATOR: They had never tasted anything so delicious in their lives as those *mele.* Katinka determined that she would go to the forest and find that *mele* tree and whether or not she was allowed to, she would shake the tree so hard that all the *mele* would be hers!

> *(KATINKA rushes out the door while STEPMOTHER tries to stop her.)*

NARRATOR: Her mother tried to stop her but a spoiled child listens to nothing. Everything was covered with snow and Katinka soon lost her way.

> *(LIGHTS DOWN. FOREST LIGHT ON. MONTHS enter and sit or stand silently. KATINKA approaches them.)*

GENNAIO: *(Gruffly.)* Why have you come here?
KATINKA: Shut up, old fool!

> *(She rushes past them, pushing the MONTHS out of her way. GENNAIO frowns and raises his staff above his head. SOUND & LIGHT EFFECTS of storm as KATINKA stumbles about in the storm and eventually falls down and dies. MONTHS cover her with white blanket of snow. SOUND & LIGHT EFFECTS DIMINISH.)*

NARRATOR: When Katinka did not return, her mother decided to go and look for her.

(SOUND & LIGHT EFFECTS as STEPMOTHER goes out in the storm, stumbles around and eventually falls down and dies. MONTHS cover her with a blanket of snow. SOUND & LIGHT EFFECTS STOP.)

NARRATOR: Dobrunka waited for them but they never returned. She remained sole mistress of the house, the garden, and the cow.

(DOBRUNKA enters the house.)

NARRATOR: The Twelve Months did not abandon their child. More than once, when the north wind blew fearfully, old *gennaio* stopped up all the crevices of the house with snow, so that the cold might not enter her home.

(GENNAIO enters and pantomimes the above.)

NARRATOR: Dobrunka lived to a good and happy old age, always having, according to the proverb:
Winter at the door,

(GENNAIO & other WINTER MONTHS enter.)

Summer in the barn,

(GIUGNO & other SUMMER MONTHS enter.)

Autumn in the cellar,

(SETTEMBRE & other AUTUMN MONTHS enter.)

and Spring in the heart.

(MARZO & other SPRING MONTHS enter.)

ALL: The end!

(LIGHTS DOWN.)

APPENDIX A: VOCABULARY LIST
OF FOREIGN LANGUAGE

ITALIAN	ENGLISH	PRONUNCIATION
arrivederci	good-bye	ah-ree-veh-dare'-chee
avanti	hurry	ah-vahn'-tee
fanciulla mia	my child (feminine)	fahn-choo'-lah mee'-ah
fanciullo mio	my child (masculine)	fahn-choo'-lo mee'-o
fragole	strawberries	frah'-go-leh
fratello	brother	frah-tel'-lo
grazie	thank you	grah'-tz'yeah
I Dodici Mesi	The Twelve Months	ee doh'-dee chee meh'-zee
la montagna	the mountain	lah mohn-tahn'-yah
mele	apples	meh'-leh
sì	yes	see
sorella	sister	soh-rel'-ah
violette	violets	vee-o-leh'-teh

	Mesi (Months):	
gennaio	January	jen-i'-o
febbraio	February	feh-bri'-o
marzo	March	mahr'-tzo
aprile	April	ah-pree'-leh
maggio	May	mah'-jo
giugno	June	june'-yoh
luglio	July	loo'-lyo
agosto	August	ah-go'-sto
settembre	September	seh-tehm'-breh
ottobre	October	oh-to'-breh
novembre	November	no-vehm'-breh
dicembre	December	dee-chem'-breh
		(hard "ch")

NOTE: In Italian, roll all the "r's" whenever possible

SETS LIST

HOUSE INTERIOR:
2 chairs
freestanding wall of house interior (optional)
doorway (optional)

MOUNTAIN/FOREST:
1 or more sturdy tables
slides, chairs, or other access to tabletops
dark cloths to hang from tabletops to the floor (optional)
sturdy tape (as needed)
freestanding wall or other backdrop of winter forest scene
freestanding wall of spring and summer backdrops (reversible)
apple tree (freestanding)
fire pit

HOW TO MAKE THE SETS

FREE-STANDING WALLS (for house interior and forest season scenes)
- very large, cardboard box
- cardboard cutting knife
- scissors
- heavy butcher paper
- tape or glue
- markers, crayons or paint with brushes
- colored paper or fabric (optional)

Cut box to create a freestanding wall with accordion folds. Cut butcher paper to size of the wall. Tape or glue paper to one or both sides of the wall (if cardboard is plain white, you can eliminate this step). Draw picture of the backdrop on the wall with markers, crayons, or paint. Colored paper or fabric can also be used to decorate the wall, using glue or tape.

LANDSCAPE BACKDROP
- heavy butcher paper
- markers, crayons or paint with brushes
- sturdy tape
- scissors

Cut butcher paper to fit across upstage wall. Draw scenes of the house interior or forest with markers, crayons, or paint. Make sure the artists understand which end is up and that drawings must be large enough to be seen from the audience. Tape to wall.

MOUNTAIN

- 1 or more sturdy tables
- ramps, stepladders or other access to tabletops
- large pieces of cloth, preferably dark
- sturdy tape

Set up tables, ramps and/or stepladders to create a hill on which the actors can move freely, up and down. Arrange the furniture at various angles, if possible. Tables with legs that fold underneath can be made into ramps: Fold under one end of legs while extending the other end of legs. Tape cloth pieces to hang over the sides. This creates a hidden, backstage area for the actors.

APPLE TREE

- large piece of heavy cardboard
- cardboard cutting tool
- stand such as a music or microphone stand or cardboard prop
- markers, crayons or paint with brushes
- colored construction paper
- scissors
- glue
- sturdy tape (as needed)

Draw a large tree on the cardboard and cut it out. Decorate with markers, crayons, paint, and/or construction paper to make an apple tree laden with large apples. Devise a way to make the tree freestanding, such as taping it to a music or microphone stand or other freestanding pole, or by creating a prop for it out of heavy cardboard.

FIRE PIT

- several cardboard paper towel tubes or other cardboard pieces, rolled like logs
- flat piece of cardboard, approx. 30 cm. square
- red, orange and/or yellow tissue paper
- clear tape

Tape the tubes or other, log-shaped pieces of cardboard to the flat piece of cardboard. Tear the tissue paper into large pieces, stick them under and around the logs and tape with clear tape so that they jut up and out like flames.

APPENDIX C: PROPS

PROPS LIST

Broom
Violets

Strawberries
2 Apples (real, plastic or papeer mâché)
Basket
Staff (can decorate with feathers, glitter, and so on)
2 Blankets of Snow (white cloth)

HOW TO MAKE THE PROPS

VIOLETS

- violet tissue or other paper (tissue is best)
- scissors
- ruler
- pencil
- clear tape
- green pipe cleaners

Measure and cut several squares of the paper, each approximately 8-10 cm square. Layer 3-4 squares on top of the other, with the points of the squares going in different directions. Place the eraser end of the pencil in the center of the squares and twist the paper around the pencil end. Remove the pencil and twist the paper center while fluffing out the edges of the squares. Tape the twisted paper point to the end of a pipe cleaner. A dozen or so violets should be plenty.

STRAWBERRIES

- red tissue or other paper (tissue is best)
- scissors
- clear tape

Cut a square of the paper, approximately 10-15 cm square. Wad it up to form a strawberry shape and tape together. The strawberries should be fairly large. A dozen or so strawberries should be plenty.

APPLES

- newspaper or butcher paper
- tape
- flour, salt & water – or other papier mâché mixture
- bowl
- red or green paint
- paint brushes

To make papier mâché apples: Wad up the paper to form two large, apple-sized balls. Wrap tape around the balls to secure their shape. Mix up flour, lots of salt, and a little water to form a gloopy mixture with the consistency of pancake batter. Tear up some paper into strips, approximately 3-5 cm wide and 30 cm long. Dip the strips into the papier mâché mixture, wipe off the excess, and layer the strips around the balls until they're completely covered. Allow several days to dry completely. Paint red or green.

APPENDIX D: COSTUMES

DOBRUNKA, KATINKA & STEPMOTHER: plain skirts or dresses, may include head scarves or aprons. Dobrunka wears poorer looking clothes than the others.

12 MONTHS: Anything goes – the actors can create their own ideas of how each month should be represented. If you have limited time and resources, they can wear plain, solid color or black clothes, accented with colored scarves tied in any fashion.

APPENDIX E: SOUND & MUSIC

Sound: Magic and Snowstorm: percussion instruments, noisemakers
Song: *"I Dodici Mesi"* (included)

I DODICI MESI
("The Twelve Months")

THE LITTLE RED HEN

This play is highly adaptable to all kinds of situations and can be produced with a short amount of preparation time or performed impromptu. The version of this tale most familiar to us is about a Hen, a Cat, a Dog, and a Mouse. They all live together in one house and the subject of the action is the growing and harvesting of wheat which is made into bread in the end.

I've introduced a few changes in this story, in order to make the play production more adaptable. Instead of only four characters, all the roles can be played as small groups so that lots of actors can be in the play. (I've labeled the characters as singular for simplicity's sake – alter the script as needed.) I've set each scene at a different season and holiday in order to trace the entire growing season, to create a holiday play, and to make each scene unique and interesting. I've selected pumpkins to be the crop because they are more visible and easier to get or make than wheat stalks and to make this a Thanksgiving holiday play. In this play, the animals all live in different houses in order to make it easier to stage – each character or group of characters can be assigned a different area of the stage or room.

This play can be altered even more, if desired. The following are some suggested variations (change the script as needed):

The actors can select any animal they would like to be, not limited to hens, cats, dogs and mice. There can also be more or less than four sets of animals.

The play can be set in another country or culture, possibly with the inclusion of a foreign language (see Appendix A for a list of some foreign language possibilities). Instead of American holidays, such as July 4, the animals could celebrate holidays particular to that country or culture, or perhaps the Hen prepares the meals for other occasions such as birthdays.

The principal crop can be anything that requires planting, watering, harvesting, and making into a food product. If you set this play in another country or culture, the food crop and holiday can be altered to suit, such as:

China – rice – sticky rice cakes for Chinese New Year's

Native America (North, Central or South) – corn – cornmeal cakes for a harvest celebration

Judaism – potatoes – latkes (potato pancakes) for Hanukkah.

The actors can improvise excuses why they can't possibly help with the chores, such as "I have to go to a birthday party" or "I have to go brush my teeth." If working with groups of characters, perhaps one actor can be assigned the line for each scene, or they can all agree on the excuses beforehand so that they can say their lines together.

Because the main action of the story revolves around the growing season, this play can be integrated with a teaching unit on the seasons or the growing cycle of plants. It can also work with a unit about a certain culture or holiday. Each season or holiday can be illustrated with a special backdrop and/or props.

I recommend pantomiming eating and drinking and not using food and drink props because the actors can easily get distracted by them. Another idea is to act out this play during snack time and have the actors actually eat in each scene.

RUNNING TIME OF SHOW: *(approximate)*
 15-20 minutes
REHEARSAL TIME NEEDED:
 4-6 hours
OTHER PRODUCTION TIME NEEDED:
 1-3 hours
CAST SIZE:
 Minimum: 4, plus Narrator
 Maximum: 25-30
GENDER OF CHARACTERS:
 All characters can be played as either female or male, with the obvious exception of "Hen."

CHARACTERS: (May substitute any animals and/or groups of animals.)
 NARRATOR
 LITTLE RED HEN
 CAT
 DOG
 MOUSE

SCENE 1: SPRING / VERNAL EQUINOX

(Setting: The house of the HEN, center, and the surrounding neighborhood which includes the homes of the other ANIMALS, located in various places around the performance space. In the HEN'S house there is a dining table and, if the cast is not too large, chairs set around it. There may be a tablecloth and flower arrangement on the table and a watering can is nearby. There may be other furniture in the house and possibly an interior wall. Off to one side is the kitchen area, including an oven and a serving tray and possibly an interior wall, other kitchen furniture and/or props. There is a front door into the house which can be indicated by two chairs or simply pantomimed. The door has either a doorbell or something to knock on, or sound effects can be made from backstage. Outside the house is the garden which may have a backdrop and/or gardening props. There are pumpkin vines and pumpkins backstage. Each of the homes of the other animals may have furniture or other sets, but it's not necessary. All the ANIMALS are in their respective homes. LIGHTS UP.)

NARRATOR: Once upon a time there lived a Little Red Hen.

(HEN enters kitchen and pantomimes cooking.)

NARRATOR: She was a terrific cook. One day, when the ground was warm and dark and ready for planting, the Little Red Hen prepared a wonderful meal to celebrate the first day of spring, which is called the Vernal Equinox. The Hen had many friends and whenever she cooked up something special they all knew it, for the delicious smells drifted all over the neighborhood. Dog, with his keen sniffer, was the first to notice. He decided to pay a call on the Little Red Hen.

(DOG comes out of his house, goes to the HEN'S door, and knocks or rings. HEN comes to the door.)

DOG: Hello, Little Red Hen!
HEN: Hello, Dog!
DOG: Please, may I stay for supper?
HEN: Sure!
DOG: Thanks!

(They go into the house.)

NARRATOR: Just then, their friend, Cat, came calling.

(CAT comes out of her house, goes to HEN'S door, and knocks or rings. HEN comes to the door.)

CAT: Hello, Little Red Hen!
HEN: Hello, Cat!
CAT: Please, may I stay for supper?
HEN: Sure!
CAT: Thanks!

(They go into the house.)

NARRATOR: Now another, hungry friend, Mouse, came by.

(MOUSE comes out of his house, goes to HEN'S door, and knocks or rings bell. HEN answers the door.)

MOUSE: Hello, Little Red Hen!
HEN: Hello, Mouse!
MOUSE: Please, may I stay for supper?
HEN: Sure!
MOUSE: Thanks!

(They go into the house. HEN goes to the kitchen and gets some food – may pantomime – while the other ANIMALS wait at the table. HEN brings in a tray of food and they all eat.)

NARRATOR: The friends all ate a wonderful meal together and when they were finished, the Hen got out some pumpkin seeds.

(HEN does so.)

HEN: Who will help me plant my pumpkin seeds?
DOG: Not I! *(May give a phony excuse.)* Good-bye!

(DOG exits.)

CAT: Not I! *(May give a phony excuse.)* Good-bye!

(CAT exits.)

MOUSE: Not I! *(May give a phony excuse.)* Good-bye!

(MOUSE exits.)

HEN: Then I'll have to do it all by myself!

NARRATOR: And so the Little Red Hen went out to her garden all by herself and planted the pumpkin seeds in the rich, brown soil.

(HEN does so. LIGHTS DOWN.)

SCENE 2: SUMMER / FOURTH OF JULY

(Setting: The same, a few months later. HEN is in her garden, all the other ANIMALS are in their respective homes. LIGHTS UP.)

NARRATOR: Three months later, the pumpkin vines had grown long and green.

(HEN pulls vine props onto stage then goes into her house.)

NARRATOR: It was time for the Fourth of July and to celebrate, the Little Red Hen cooked a fabulous supper. The Dog sniffed those good smells and decided it was time to pay another visit to the Hen.

(Repeat same sequence as in Scene 1: Each ANIMAL in turn comes to HEN'S door, asks to stay for supper and is invited in. NARRATOR can announce each ANIMAL'S entrance, if needed. HEN brings in a tray of food from the kitchen and they all eat.)

NARRATOR: When they were finished eating, the Hen got out her watering can.

(HEN does so.)

HEN: Who will help me water my pumpkin plants?

DOG: Not I! *(May give a phony excuse.)* Good-bye!

(DOG exits.)

CAT: Not I! *(May give a phony excuse.)* Good-bye!

(CAT exits.)

MOUSE: Not I! *(May give a phony excuse.)* Good-bye!

(MOUSE exits.)

HEN: Then I'll have to do it all by myself!

NARRATOR: And so the Little Red Hen went out to her garden alone and gave her pumpkin vines a big drink of cool, clear water.

(HEN does so. LIGHTS DOWN.)

SCENE 3: AUTUMN/HALLOWEEN

(Setting: The same, a few months later. All the ANIMALS are in their respective homes. LIGHTS UP.)

NARRATOR: By October, the pumpkin vines were sprouting big, orange pumpkins which shone in the autumn sunlight.

(HEN places pumpkins onto vines then goes into her house.)

NARRATOR: At the end of the month, the Little Red Hen prepared a feast to celebrate Halloween. As usual, whenever the Hen cooked up some fine food, Dog made a point of coming by for a visit.

(Repeat same sequence as in Scenes 1 & 2: Each ANIMAL in turn comes to HEN'S door, asks to stay for supper and is invited in. NARRATOR can announce each ANIMAL'S entrance, if needed. HEN brings in a tray of food from the kitchen and they all eat.)

NARRATOR: When they were finished eating, the Hen asked:
HEN: Who will help me harvest my pumpkins?
DOG: Not I! *(May give a phony excuse.)* Good-bye!

(DOG exits.)

CAT: Not I! *(May give a phony excuse.)* Good-bye!

(CAT exits.)

MOUSE: Not I! *(May give a phony excuse.)* Good-bye!

(MOUSE exits.)

HEN: Then I'll have to do it all by myself!
NARRATOR: And so the Little Red Hen went out to her garden alone and harvested her pumpkins.

(HEN does so and puts the pumpkins in the kitchen. LIGHTS DOWN.)

SCENE 4: THANKSGIVING DAY

(Setting: The same, Thanksgiving Day. The ANIMALS are all in their respective homes. LIGHTS UP.)

NARRATOR: It was now Thanksgiving Day. The Hen was busy cleaning her house and preparing for the feast. Her guests were so impatient to eat her good cooking they showed up several hours early.

(DOG comes out of his house, goes to HEN'S house, and knocks or rings the bell. HEN answers the door.)

DOG: Happy Thanksgiving, Hen!
HEN: I'm not ready yet! Well, come in anyway.
DOG: Thanks!

(They go into the house. CAT comes out of her house, goes to HEN'S house, and knocks or rings the bell. HEN answers the door.)

CAT: Happy Thanksgiving, Hen!
HEN: I'm not ready yet! Well, come in anyway.
CAT: Thanks!

(They go into the house. MOUSE comes out of his house, goes to HEN'S house, and knocks or rings the bell. HEN answers the door.)

MOUSE: Happy Thanksgiving, Hen!
HEN: I'm not ready yet! Well, come in anyway.
MOUSE: Thanks!

(They go into the house.)

NARRATOR: The Hen was ready to begin baking the pies.
HEN: Who will help me bake my pumpkin pies?
DOG: Not I! *(May give a phony excuse, but does not exit.)*
CAT: Not I! *(May give a phony excuse but does not exit.)*
MOUSE: Not I! *(May give a phony excuse, but does not exit.)*
HEN: Then I'll have to do it all by myself!
NARRATOR: And so the Little Red Hen went into her kitchen and made beautiful, golden, pumpkin pies.

(HEN goes into the kitchen and pantomimes making pies.)

NARRATOR: The delicious smell of the pies baking in the oven floated all over the house and Dog, Cat, and Mouse went crazy waiting to eat them! Soon it was time for Thanksgiving dinner.

(HEN brings in a tray of food and they all eat.)

NARRATOR: When everyone had eaten, the Hen brought out the pumpkin pies.

(HEN does so.)

HEN: Who will help me eat my pumpkin pies?
ALL: I WILL!! I WILL!!
HEN: NO! You did not help me plant the seeds. You did not help me water the plants. You did not help me harvest the pumpkins. And you did not help me bake the pies! So why should I let you eat them?
NARRATOR: And with that, the Little Red Hen ate all the pies by herself, while the others watched sadly.

(They do so.)

NARRATOR: But the next time the Hen asked for help, Dog, Cat, and Mouse had learned their lesson.
HEN: Who will help me wash the dishes?
ALL: I WILL!! I WILL!!

(May add song/dance here.)

NARRATOR: The end!

(LIGHTS DOWN.)

APPENDIX A: VOCABULARY LIST OF
FOREIGN LANGUAGE WORDS (suggested)

ENGLISH
FRENCH
SPANISH
GERMAN
RUSSIAN
  (spelled with Latin alphabet)
CHINESE
  (spelled with Latin alphabet)

yes
oui ("wee")
si ("see")
ja ("yah")
da ("dah")
hau ("how" – lift voice slightly at the
  end)

no
non ("noh")
no
nein ("nine")
nyet
bù ("boo")

hello
bonjour ("bohn-jhoor'")
hola ("oh'-lah")
guten tag ("goo-ten tahk'")
privyet ("pree-vyet'")
ni-hao ("nee'-how")

good-bye
au revoir ("oh reh-vwah'")
adios ("ah-dee-ohs'")
auf Wiedersehen ("off vee'-duh-zane")
dosvedanya ("doe-svee-don'-yah")
zài-jiàn ("dz'eye jyen'")

please
s'il vous plâit ("see voo play'")
por favor ("pour fah-vor'")
pujahlsta ("puh-jhahl'-eh'stuh")
ching ("ching" – lift voice slightly in
  the middle)

thank you
merci ("mare-see'")
gracias ("grah'-see-ahs")]
spaseeba ("spah-see'-buh")
xìe-xìe ("shay'-shay")

SETS LIST

HEN'S HOUSE:
 large table
 oven (can use a decorated cardboard box)
 doorway (optional – can use 2 chairs)
 interior walls (optional)
 chairs (optional)
 other furniture (optional)

GARDEN:
 landscape backdrop (optional)

OTHER ANIMAL HOUSES (optional):
 chairs
 tables
 interior walls

HOW TO MAKE THE SETS

FREESTANDING WALLS (for house interior and garden landscape)
- very large cardboard box
- cardboard cutting knife
- scissors
- heavy butcher paper
- tape or glue
- markers, crayons or paint with brushes
- colored paper or fabric (optional)

Cut box to create a freestanding wall with accordion folds. Cut a piece of butcher paper to size of the wall. Tape or glue paper to the wall (if cardboard is plain white, you can eliminate this step). Draw picture of the set on the wall with markers, crayons, or paint. Colored paper or fabric can also be used to decorate the wall, using glue or tape.

LANDSCAPE BACKDROP
- heavy butcher paper
- markers, crayons or paint with brushes
- sturdy tape
- scissors

Cut butcher paper to fit across upstage wall. Draw scenes of the Hen's garden with markers, crayons, or paint. Make sure the artists understand which end is up and that drawings must be large enough to be seen from the audience. Tape to wall.

PROPS LIST

Serving Tray
Pumpkin Seeds (optional)
Pumpkin Vines
Pumpkins (real or made)
Pumpkin Pies (real or orange paper fitted into pie tins)
Food & Drink Props (optional)
Table Cloth (Optional)
Flower Arrangement (Optional)
Gardening Tools (Optional)

HOW TO MAKE THE PROPS

PUMPKIN VINES
- string
- green construction paper
- scissors
- tape

Fold the paper into thirds or quarters. Draw leaves on the paper including stems and cut out so that several leaves are cut out at once. Cut 3-4 lengths of string, 2-3 meters long each and tape the leaf stems onto the string.

PUMPKINS
- several, medium-sized paper sacks
- old newspapers or other stuffing
- stapler
- orange paint
- paintbrushes

Indent the corners of the bags and staple inside to make a more spherical shape. Stuff the bags with newspaper or other, light stuffing and staple at the top, again, shaping into a sphere. Paint orange.

APPENDIX D: COSTUMES

ALL: plain, colored pants & shirt or leotard & tights, with ears and tails.

HOW TO MAKE THE COSTUMES

ANIMAL EARS
- colored construction paper
- pencil
- scissors
- stapler
- light cardboard, glue (optional)
- markers, crayons, paint with brushes, (optional)
- fake fur, glue (optional)

Draw and cut out shape of animal ears with pencil on appropriate color of paper. Cut long strips of the same colors, approximately 4 cm wide and long enough to go around the actors' heads with a 2-3 centimeters of overlap. Staple ears to strips, and staple strips to fit snugly around the actors' heads. You may want to reinforce ears and strips with a cardboard backing. Decorate as needed with markers, crayons, paint, or bits of fake fur.

ANIMAL TAILS
- long strips, approx. 1 meter long, of colored chiffon or other light fabric
- scissors
- long, elastic strip or safety pins

Measure out three strips of fabric. Braid together and tie in a knot at either end. Tail is either pinned to back of actor's pants or tied to an elastic strip that is measured and tied to fit around actor's waist. The best place to pin the tail to pants is through belt loops. If you pin it directly to pants or shirt, it can rip the fabric if someone steps on the tail.

HEN FEATHERS:
- feathers
- tape
- long, elastic strip

Measure and tie the elastic to fit around the actor's waist. Tape the feathers to the back of the elastic. You can also do a similar thing around the actor's head.

APPENDIX E: SOUND & MUSIC

SOUND:
> wood blocks or bells for Hen's door

MUSIC:
> Thanksgiving song or folksong from another country or culture (optional – see other plays in this volume for some ideas).

THE LONG LEATHER BAG
(Ireland)

This tale comes to us from Ireland. The Irish language is called Gaelic. Various forms of Gaelic are or were also spoken in Scotland and the Isle of Man. Gaelic is the official first language of the Republic of Ireland and it is taught in the schools; however, except for some Gaelic-speaking enclaves in a few remote parts of the country and in some official political, educational, and bureaucratic circles in the capital, Dublin, most modern Irish people use English as their primary language.

"Hag" originally meant "holy woman." Hags have appeared in traditions and religions as *Hecate* (Old Greek), *The Hag of the Iron Wood* (Old Norse), *The Hag of Scone* (Denmark), and *Hagazussa* (Old German), to name a few. Hags are powerful because they rule Death—as does the Cailleach of this story. When death is feared it becomes regarded as evil; thus has the term "hag" declined from it's original holy status.

This story, like so many from our European heritage, is based on repetition and the number three (three Daughters) and the number seven (seven years since the animals and mill have been tended). The repetitiveness of scenes and lines makes it easier for the actors to learn and remember their parts. If you have a large cast, the animals can be played by small groups of actors, and this also makes it easier for them to learn and remember what to do and say. It also provides support for the shyest actors who may feel uncomfortable playing a role all by themselves. The plural forms of the Gaelic for the animal characters are noted in the script and in the vocabulary list in Appendix A.

It's helpful for the actors if there is a consistent pathway to follow in the blocking. The animals can be pushed out of the way gently—the actor being pushed actually does the work of moving. Or, instead of pushing them, Eldest and Second Daughter can throw paper stones at the animals (that is, if your cast can control themselves!)

When copying script pages for the actors, you can save paper by giving the Cailleach, the animals and the Muileann scenes 2, 3 & 4 and instructing them that these scenes for the Eldest Daughter – scenes 5,

6, & 7 – are exactly the same for the Second Daughter. It's also possible to shorten the length of the play by eliminating scenes 5,6 & 7.

RUNNING TIME OF SHOW: *(approximate)*
    15-25 minutes
REHEARSAL TIME NEEDED:
    8-10 hours
OTHER PRODUCTION TIME NEEDED:
    3-4 hours
CAST SIZE:
    Minimum: 10, plus Narrator
    Maximum: 25-30 (Animals and Muileann can each be played by small groups.)
GENDER OF CHARACTERS:
    Mathair, Daughters, and Cailleach are traditionally portrayed as females, but it may be possible to play them as males. The Animals and the Muileann can be played as either female or male.

CHARACTERS:
    NARRATOR
    MATHAIR — Mother
    ELDEST DAUGHTER
    SECOND DAUGHTER
    YOUNGEST DAUGHTER
    CAILLEACH — Hag or Dark Witch
    MUILEANN — Mill
    CAPALL/CAPAILL —Horse (singular/plural)
    CAORA/CAOIRIGH — Sheep (singular/plural)
    GABHAR/GABHAIR — Goat (feminine form; singular/plural
    BÓ/BA — Cow (singular/plural)

SCENE 1

(Setting: Ireland, in days long ago. In one area of the stage is a grassy hill, in another area is a mill, and in another area is the interior of Mathair's house, including a chair and an interior wall wiht a fireplace painted on it. There is a hatch in the wall where the fireplace is, through which to pass props. Three bannocks are hidden in the fireplace, and nearby are three traveling bags. NARRATOR, MATHAIR & DAUGHTERS enter. MATHAIR holds a long leather bag. She sits in the chair and her DAUGHTERS gather around her. LIGHTS UP.)

NARRATOR: *Fadó, fadó in Eireanna.* Long, long ago in Ireland, there lived a widow and her three daughters. When their father died, he had left them a long leather bag full of *ór* and *airgead,* gold and silver, and so they thought they would never be poor.

(MATHAIR and DAUGHTERS inspect the bag. CAILLEACH enters and knocks at their door. MATHAIR goes to the door.)

MATHAIR: *Dia dhuit.* Good day.

CAILLEACH: *Dia dhuit.* Might ye have a bite to eat for a poor, old woman?

MATHAIR: *Ta.* Wait here. Come, children!

(MATHAIR & DAUGHTERS exit. CAILLEACH sneaks around the house, sees the bag and looks inside.)

CAILLEACH: *Ór* and *airgead!!* Gold and silver! 'Tis the luck of the Irish!

(She takes the bag, and exits, running. MATHAIR & DAUGHTERS enter.)

ALL: Our long leather bag is gone!

MATHAIR: Stop that thief!

(MATHAIR & DAUGHTERS chase CAILLEACH, but she escapes.)

ALL: What will we do now?!!

(LIGHTS DOWN.)

SCENE 2

(Setting: Same, seven years later. MATHAIR is in her chair with her DAUGHTERS around her. LIGHTS UP.)

NARRATOR: In the years following the loss of their long leather bag, the widow and her daughters were very poor and had a hard life. When seven years had passed, the Eldest Daughter came and spoke to her *Mathair.*

ELDEST: *Mathair,* I'm grown up now and 'tis a shame I'm doing nothing to help you or myself. Bake me a bannock and cut me a callop, 'till I go away to push my fortune.

NARRATOR: So her *Mathair* baked her a bannock, a round, flat loaf of bread.

(MATHAIR goes to fireplace, gets bannock. Hidden actor can pass it to her through the hatch in the fireplace set.)

MATHAIR: Will you have *half* of it with my blessing or the *whole* of it *without?*

ELDEST: I'll take the *whole* bannock *without* your blessing.

(MATHAIR gives her bannock which she puts in a traveling bag.)

ELDEST: If I'm not back in a year and a day, you will know I am doing well and making my fortune! *Slán abhaile!*

MATHAIR, SECOND & YOUNGEST: *Slán abhaile!*

(ELDEST exits. LIGHTS DOWN. Change set: Replace Mathair's house with Cailleach's hut.)

SCENE 3

(Setting: Cailleach's hut interior, including chair and interior wall with a fireplace painted on it. This is the reverse side of MATHAIR'S house interior wall and uses the same fireplace hatch for passing props. There is a broom by the hearth, the long leather bag is hidden behind the fireplace, and a long, white rod is nearby. LIGHTS UP. ELDEST enters and travels over hill and all around while NARRATOR speaks the following.)

NARRATOR: She traveled away and away, far further than I could tell you, and twice as far as you could tell me, until she came to a strange country. There she found a little hut where lived an old *Cailleach*, an old hag.

(ELDEST comes to hut and knocks on the door. CAILLEACH enters and comes to the door.)

ELDEST: *Dia dhuit.*

CAILLEACH: *Dia dhuit.* Where are you going?

ELDEST: I'm going to push my fortune.

CAILLEACH: Would you like to stay here with me? I need a maid.

ELDEST: What will I have to do?

CAILLEACH: You will have to wash me and dress me and sweep the hearth clean, but on the peril of your life, NEVER LOOK UP THE CHIMNEY!

ELDEST: *Ta.*

(She enters the hut. LIGHTS DOWN.)

SCENE 4

(Setting: Same, the next morning. ELDEST is sweeping hearth, CAILLEACH stands nearby. LIGHTS UP.)

NARRATOR: The next day, the Eldest Daughter washed and dressed the *Cailleach*, and when the old hag went out she swept the hearth clean.

(CAILLEACH exits.)

NARRATOR: She thought it would do no harm to have one wee look up the chimney...

(She looks up the chimney, gasps, and pulls out the long, leather bag. Hidden actor can pass it to her through the hatch in the fireplace set.)

ELDEST: My *Mathair's* long leather bag!

(She runs out of the hut.)

NARRATOR: She had not gone far when she met a *capall*, a horse (OR: *capaill*, horses).

(CAPALL enters, blocks her way.)

CAPALL: Oh, rub me! Rub me! For I haven't been rubbed these seven years!

ELDEST: Get out of my way!

(She pushes CAPALL out of her way and runs toward the hill as CAORA enters, on top of the hill.)

NARRATOR: She had not gone much farther when she met a *caora*, a sheep [OR: *caoirigh*, sheep, plural] on top of a grassy hill.

(ELDEST runs up hill, CAORA blocks her way.)

CAORA: Oh, shear me! Shear me! For I haven't been shorn these seven years!

ELDEST: Get out of my way!

(She pushes CAORA out of her way and runs down the hill as GABHAR enters near bottom of the hill.)

NARRATOR: At the bottom of the hill she met a tethered *gabhar*, a goat (OR: *gabhair*, goats).

(GABHAR blocks her way.)

GABHAR: Oh, change my tether! Change my tether! For it hasn't been changed these seven years!

ELDEST: Get out of my way!

(She pushes GABHAR out of her way and continues on as BÓ enters.)

NARRATOR: She ran on and on until she came across a *bó*, a cow *(OR: ba, cows).*

(BÓ blocks her way.)

BÓ: Oh, milk me! Milk me! For I haven't been milked these seven years!

ELDEST: Get out of my way!

(She pushes BÓ out of her way and continues on toward the MUILEANN.)

NARRATOR: Before long she came to a *muileann*, a mill.

MUILEANN: Oh, turn me! Turn me! For I haven't been turned these seven years!

NARRATOR: Not bothering to answer the *muileann* the Eldest Daughter went inside and, using the long leather bag as a pillow, lay down and went to sleep.

(She climbs to top of mill, lays down with bag under her head, and sleeps.)

NARRATOR: Soon the Cailleach came home and discovered that the girl was gone. First thing, she looked up the chimney.

(She does so and sees that the bag is missing.)

CAILLEACH: AAARRGGHH!!!

(She grabs her white rod and runs of the hut. She comes upon the CAPALL.)

CAILLEACH: Oh, *capall, capall* o' mine, (OR: *capaill*)
did you see this maid o' mine,
with my tig, with my tag,
with my long leather bag,
and all the *ór* and *airgead*
I have earned since I was a maid?
CAPALL: 'Tis not long since she passed here.

(CAPALL exits. CAILLEACH runs up the hill to where CAORA is.)

CAILLEACH: Oh, *caora, caora* o' mine, (OR: *caoirigh*)
did you see this maid o' mine,
with my tig, with my tag,
with my long leather bag,
and all the *ór* and *airgead*
I have earned since I was a maid?
CAORA: 'Tis not long since she passed here.

(CAORA exits. CAILLEACH runs down the hill to where GABHAR is.)

CAILLEACH: Oh, *gabhar, gabhar* o' mine, (OR: *gabhair*)
did you see this maid o' mine,
with my tig, with my tag,
with my long leather bag,

and all the *ór* and *airgead*
I have earned since I was a maid?
GABHAR: 'Tis not long since she passed here.

(GABHAR exits. CAILLEACH runs to where BÓ is.)

CAILLEACH: Oh, *bó, bó* o' mine, (OR: *ba*)
did you see this maid o' mine,
with my tig, with my tag,
with my long leather bag,
and all the *ór* and *airgead*
I have earned since I was a maid?
BÓ: 'Tis not long since she passed here.

(BÓ exits. CAILLEACH runs to the MUILEANN.)

CAILLEACH: Oh, *muileann, muileann* o' mine,
did you see this maid o' mine,
with my tig, with my tag,
with my long leather bag,
and all the *ór* and *airgead*
I have earned since I was a maid?
MUILEANN: *Ta.* She's sleeping behind the door.

(CAILLEACH climbs to top of mill.)

NARRATOR: The Cailleach struck the Eldest Daughter with her white rod and turned her into a stone.

(SOUND & LIGHTS EFFECTS as CAILLEACH strikes ELDEST who freezes into stone. A large prop stone is placed in the mill or lowered from a pulley into place while the actor slips backstage. CAILLEACH takes the bag from under her head and returns to her hut, then exits. LIGHTS DOWN. Change set: Replace CAILLEACH'S hut with MATHAIR'S house.)

(NOTE: For a shorter version of this play, skip the following scene and replace with:)

NARRATOR: When a year and a day had passed, the Second Daughter of the widow went out to push her fortune with a whole bannock but without her *mathair's* blessing. The Second Daughter also met up with the *Cailleach* and repeated the same fate as her sister before her. She too found her *mathair's* long leather bag in the hag's chimney and tried to escape with it. But like her sister, she was not kind to the animals and the *muillean* and so the *Cailleach* was able to find her and change her into a stone.

(Place second stone in mill and skip to SCENE 8.)

SCENE 5

(Setting: MATHAIR'S house, as before. MATHAIR, SECOND & YOUNGEST DAUGHTERS enter. LIGHTS UP.)

NARRATOR: When a year and a day had passed and the Eldest Daughter had not returned, the Second Daughter came and spoke to her *mathair.*

SECOND: *Mathair,* my sister has not returned and 'tis a shame I'm doing nothing to help you or myself. Bake me a bannock and cut me a callop 'til I go away to push my fortune.

(MATHAIR goes to fireplace, gets bannock.)

MATHAIR: Will you have *half* of it *with* my blessing or the *whole* of it *without?*

SECOND: I'll take the *whole* bannock *without* your blessing.

(MATHAIR gives her bannock which she puts in a traveling bag.)

SECOND: If I'm not back in a year and a day, you will know I am doing well and making my fortune! *Slán abhaile!*

MATHAIR & YOUNGEST: *Slán abhaile!*

(SECOND Exits. LIGHTS DOWN. Change set: Replace MATH-AIR'S house with CAILLEACH'S hut.)

SCENE 6

(Setting: Cailleach's hut, as before. LIGHTS UP. SECOND enters and travels over hill and all around while NARRATOR speaks the following.)

NARRATOR: She traveled away and away, far further than I could tell you, and twice as far as you could tell me, until she came to the hut of the old *Cailleach.*

(SECOND comes to hut and knocks on the door. CAILLEACH enters and comes to the door.)

SECOND: *Dia dhuit.*

CAILLEACH: *Dia dhuit.* Where are you going?

SECOND: I'm going to push my fortune.

CAILLEACH: Would you like to stay here with me? I need a maid.

SECOND: What will I have to do?

CAILLEACH: You will have to wash me and dress me and sweep the hearth clean, but on the peril of your life, NEVER LOOK UP THE CHIMNEY!

SECOND: *Ta.*

(She enters the hut. LIGHTS DOWN.)

SCENE 7

(Setting: Same, the next morning. SECOND is sweeping hearth, CAILLEACH stands nearby. LIGHTS UP.)

NARRATOR: The next day, the Second Daughter washed and dressed the *Cailleach,* and when the old hag went out she swept the hearth clean.

(CAILLEACH exits.)

NARRATOR: She thought it would do no harm to have one wee look up the chimney...

(She looks up the chimney, gasps, and pulls out the long, leather bag.)

SECOND: My *Mathair's* long leather bag!

(She runs out of the hut. CAPALL enters, blocking her way.)

CAPALL: Oh, rub me! Rub me! For I haven't been rubbed these seven years!

SECOND: Get out of my way!

(She pushes CAPALL out of her way and runs toward the hill as CAORA enters, on top of hill, blocking her way.)

CAORA: Oh, shear me! Shear me! For I haven't been shorn these seven years!

SECOND: Get out of my way!

(She pushes CAORA out of her way and runs down the hill as GAB-HAR enters, blocking her way.)

GABHAR: Oh, change my tether! Change my tether! For it hasn't been changed these seven years!
SECOND: Get out of my way!

(She pushes GABHAR out of her way and continues on as BÓ enters, blocking her way.)

BÓ: Oh, milk me! Milk me! For I haven't been milked these seven years!
SECOND: Get out of my way!

(She pushes BÓ out of her way and continues on toward the MUILEANN.)

MUILEANN: Oh, turn me! Turn me! For I haven't been turned these seven years!
NARRATOR: The Second Daughter paid no heed to the *muileann* and went inside. She lay down next to a large stone and, using the long leather bag as a pillow, she went to sleep.

(She does so.)

NARRATOR: Soon the *Cailleach* came home and discovered that the girl was gone. First thing, she looked up the chimney.

(She does so and sees that the bag is missing.)

CAILLEACH: AAARRGGHH!!!

(She grabs her white rod and runs of the hut. She comes upon the CAPALL.)

CAILLEACH: Oh, *capall, capall* o' mine, (OR: *capaill*)
did you see this maid o' mine,
with my tig, with my tag,
with my long leather bag,
and all the *ór* and *airgead*
I have earned since I was a maid?
CAPALL: Ay, 'tis not long since she passed here.

(CAPALL exits. CAILLEACH runs up the hill to where CAORA is.)

CAILLEACH: Oh, *caora, caora* o' mine, (OR: *caoirigh*)
    did you see this maid o' mine,
    with my tig, with my tag,
    with my long leather bag,
    and all the *ór* and *airgead*
    I have earned since I was a maid?
CAORA: 'Tis not long since she passed here.

(CAORA exits. CAILLEACH runs down the hill to where GABHAR is.)

CAILLEACH: Oh, *gabhar, gabhar* o' mine, (OR: *gabhair*)
    did you see this maid o' mine,
    with my tig, with my tag,
    with my long leather bag,
    and all the *ór* and *airgead*
    I have earned since I was a maid?
GABHAR: 'Tis not long since she passed here.

(GABHAR exits. CAILLEACH runs to where BÓ is.)

CAILLEACH: Oh, *bó, bó* o' mine, (OR: *ba*)
    did you see this maid o' mine,
    with my tig, with my tag,
    with my long leather bag,
    and all the *ór* and *airgead*
    I have earned since I was a maid?
BÓ: 'Tis not long since she passed here.

(BÓ exits. CAILLEACH runs to the MUILEANN.)

CAILLEACH: Oh, *muileann, muileann* o' mine,
    did you see this maid o' mine,
    with my tig, with my tag,
    with my long leather bag,
    and all the *ór* and *airgead*
    I have earned since I was a maid?
MUILEANN: *Ta.* She's sleeping behind the door.

(CAILLEACH climbs to top of mill. SOUND & LIGHTS EFFECTS as CAILLEACH strikes SECOND who freezes into stone and is replaced by a prop stone. CAILLEACH takes the bag from under her

head and returns to her hut, then exits. LIGHTS DOWN. Change set: Replace CAILLEACH'S hut with MATHAIR'S house.)

SCENE 8

(Setting: MATHAIR'S house, as before. MATHAIR & YOUNGEST enter. LIGHTS UP.)

NARRATOR: When the Second Daughter had been gone a year and a day, the Youngest Daughter came and spoke to her *mathair.*

YOUNGEST: *Mathair,* my sisters have not returned and 'tis a shame I'm doing nothing to help you or myself. Bake me a bannock and cut me a callop 'till I go away to push my fortune.

(MATHAIR goes to fireplace, gets bannock.)

MATHAIR: Will you have *half* of it *with* my blessing or the *whole* of it *without?*

YOUNGEST: I'll take *half* of the bannock *with* your blessing.

(MATHAIR tears bannock in half, gives half to YOUNGEST, which she puts in her traveling bag.)

YOUNGEST: If I'm not back in a year and a day, you will know I am doing well and making my fortune! *Slán abhaile!*

MATHAIR: *Slán abhaile!*

(YOUNGEST exits. LIGHTS DOWN. Change set: Replace MATH-AIR'S house with CAILLEACH'S hut.)

SCENE 9

(Setting: CAILLEACH'S hut, as before. LIGHTS UP. YOUNGEST enters and travels over hill and all around while NARRATOR speaks the following.)

NARRATOR: She traveled away and away, far further than I could tell you, and twice as far as you could tell me, and where she ended up, I think you know.

(YOUNGEST comes to hut and knocks on the door. CAILLEACH enters and comes to the door.)

YOUNGEST: *Dia dhuit..*

CAILLEACH: *Dia dhuit.* Where are you going?

YOUNGEST: I'm going to push my fortune.

CAILLEACH: Would you like to stay here with me? I need a maid.

YOUNGEST: What will I have to do?

CAILLEACH: You will have to wash me and dress me and sweep the hearth clean, but on the peril of your life, NEVER LOOK UP THE CHIMNEY!

YOUNGEST: Maybe I will and maybe I won't.

(She enters the hut. LIGHTS DOWN.)

SCENE 10

(Setting: Same, the next morning. YOUNGEST is sweeping hearth, CAILLEACH stands nearby. LIGHTS UP.)

NARRATOR: You won't be surprised when I tell you that the next day the youngest daughter washed and dressed the *Cailleach,* and when the old hag went out she swept the hearth clean.

(CAILLEACH exits.)

NARRATOR: And being of a curious type, like her sisters, she thought it would do no harm to have one wee look up the chimney...

(She looks up the chimney, gasps, and pulls out the long, leather bag.)

YOUNGEST: Just as I suspected!

(She runs out of the hut. CAPALL enters, blocks her way.)

CAPALL: Oh, rub me! Rub me! For I haven't been rubbed these seven years!

YOUNGEST: Oh, poor *capall,* poor *capall!* I'll surely do that! (OR: *capaill*)

(She rubs CAPALL and continues toward hill as CAORA enters, blocking her way.)

CAORA: Oh, shear me! Shear me! For I haven't been shorn these seven years!

YOUNGEST: Oh, poor *caora,* poor *caora!* I'll surely do that! (OR: *caoirigh*)

(She shears CAORA and continues down hill as GABHAR enters, blocking her way.)

GABHAR: Oh, change my tether! Change my tether! For it hasn't been changed these seven years!

YOUNGEST: Oh, poor *gabhar,* poor *gabhar!* I'll surely do that! (OR: *gabhair*)

(She changes GABHAR'S tether and continues as BÓ enters, blocking her way.)

BÓ: Oh, milk me! Milk me! For I haven't been milked these seven years!

YOUNGEST: Oh, poor *bó,* poor *bó!* I'll surely do that! (OR: *ba*)

(She milks BÓ and continues to the MUILEANN.)

MUILEANN: Oh, turn me! Turn me! For I haven't been turned these seven years!

YOUNGEST: Oh, poor *muileann,* poor *muileann!* I'll surely do that!

(She turns the wheel. She goes inside, lays down next to her stone sisters with the bag under her head and goes to sleep.)

NARRATOR: I'm sure you know what happened when the *Cailleach* came home and found the girl missing.

(CAILLEACH enters, sees that YOUNGEST is gone and looks up the chimney.)

CAILLEACH: AAARRGGHH!!!

(She grabs her white rod and runs of the hut. She comes upon the CAPALL.)

CAILLEACH: Oh, *capall, capall* o' mine, (OR: *capaill*)
did you see this maid o' mine,
with my tig, with my tag,
with my long leather bag,
and all the *ór* and *airgead*
I have earned since I was a maid?

CAPALL: Do you think I have nothing to do but watch your maids for you? Go somewhere else to look for information.

(CAPALL exits. CAILLEACH runs up the hill to where CAORA is.)

CAILLEACH: Oh, *caora, caora* o' mine, (OR: *caoirigh*)
   did you see this maid o' mine,
   with my tig, with my tag,
   with my long leather bag,
   and all the *ór* and *airgead*
   I have earned since I was a maid?
CAORA: Do you think I have nothing to do but watch your maids for
you? Go somewhere else for information.

   (CAORA exits. CAILLEACH runs down the hill to where GABHAR is.)

CAILLEACH: Oh, *gabhar, gabhar* o' mine, (OR: *gabhair*)
   did you see this maid o' mine,
   with my tig, with my tag,
   with my long leather bag,
   and all the *ór* and *airgead*
   I have earned since I was a maid?
GABHAR: Do you think I have nothing to do but watch your maids
for you? Go somewhere else for information.

   (GABHAR exits. CAILLEACH runs to where BÓ is.)

CAILLEACH: Oh, *bó, bó* o' mine, (OR: *ba*)
   did you see this maid o' mine,
   with my tig, with my tag,
   with my long leather bag,
   and all the *ór* and *airgead*
   I have earned since I was a maid?
BÓ: Do you think I have nothing to do but watch your maids for you?
Go somewhere else for information.

   (BÓ exits. CAILLEACH runs to the MUILEANN.)

CAILLEACH: Oh, *muileann, muileann* o' mine,
   did you see this maid o' mine,
   with my tig, with my tag,
   with my long leather bag,
   and all the ór and airgead
   I have earned since I was a maid?
MUILEANN: Come closer and whisper to me...

   (CAILLEACH goes close to MUILEANN.)

102 The Long Leather Bag

NARRATOR: She went closer to whisper to the *muileann,* and the mill dragged her under the wheel and ground her up!

(CAILLEACH screams and drops her rod as she is ground up under the wheel – actor can slide under table or be pulled under by backstage actors. YOUNGEST comes out and watches.)

MUILEANN: *(To Youngest:)* Take this white rod and strike the two stones behind the door.

(YOUNGEST does so. Special effects as ELDEST & SECOND spring to life.)

ELDEST & YOUNGEST: You saved us!

(ALL hug, and so forth. YOUNGEST picks up the long leather bag and they all set off for home. May do a song/dance: "dTigeas A Damhsa" or other Irish folksong.)

ALL: *Deireadh!* The End!

(LIGHTS DOWN.)

APPENDIX A: VOCABULARY LIST
OF FOREIGN LANGUAGE

IRISH-GAELIC	ENGLISH	PRONUNCIATION

(NOTE: There are numerous and varied ways to pronounce Irish, depending on what area of the country you live in. This pronunciation guide offers but one of many ways to pronounce these words.)

airgead	silver	air'-uh-ged (hard "g")
bó / ba	cow / cows	bow (long "o") / bah
cailleach	hag	ka'-luch* ("a" as in "add")
caora / caoirigh	sheep / sheep (plural)	kwair'-uh / kweer'-ig
capall / capaill	horse / horses	kah'-pull **
deireadh	the end, finished	deer'-uh
Dia dhuit	hello (literally: "God be with you")	dee-ah gwit'
fadó in Eireanna	long ago in Ireland	faw-doe' ehn air'-nah
gabhar / gabhair	goat / goats	gaur **
mathair	mother	maw'-her
muileann	mill	mill'-un
ór	gold	ohr
slán abhaile	good-bye (literally: "Safe home" or "Health to you")	slahn uh-wahl'-yuh
ta	yes (literally: "It exists")	tah

"dTigeas A Damhsa" (song):
dTigeas a damhsa dam   come dance with me jig'-us uh dous'-uh dumb

"ch" sounds softly in back of throat, such as in German "ach"
*** pronounced the same for both singular and plural*

SETS LIST

MATHAIR'S HOUSE / CAILLEACH'S HUT INTERIOR:
    freestanding wall
    1 chair

GRASSY HILL:
    1-3 large, study tables
    slides, chairs, or other access to tabletops
    green fabric pieces

MILL:
    1-2 large, sturdy tables
    stepladder, chair or other access to tabletop
    large, dark cloth
    large, rotating mill wheel on a dowel
    2 large stones (paper)

OPTIONAL:
    landscape backdrop

HOW TO MAKE THE SETS

MATHAIR'S HOUSE / CAILLEACH'S HUT INTERIOR
    • very large cardboard box
    • cardboard cutting knife
    • scissors
    • heavy butcher paper
    • tape or glue
    • markers, crayons or paint with brushes
    • colored paper or fabric (optional)

Cut box to create a freestanding wall with accordion folds. Draw a square near the center, big enough to pass through bannocks and long leather bag. Cut sides and bottom of square and fold up top to create a hatch door that can open from either side. Cut 2 pieces of butcher paper to size of the wall. Tape or glue paper to both sides of the wall, including hatch. If cardboard is plain white, you can eliminate this step. Draw house interior on wall with markers, crayons, or paint. Fireplace is center, including hatch. Interior could include pictures on the wall, tables, bookcases, and so on. Cailleach's hut interior could include dried herbs, cauldron, spells books, and so forth. Colored paper or fabric can also be used to decorate the wall, using glue or tape.

GRASSY HILL
Set up tables, ramps and/or stepladders to create a hill on which the actors can move freely, up and down. Arrange the furniture at various angles, if possible. Tables with legs that fold underneath can be made into slides by folding under one

end of the legs. Tape cloth pieces to hang over the sides. This creates a hidden, backstage area for the actors.

MILL

- 1-2 sturdy tables
- stepladder or other access to tabletop
- large piece of plain or dark fabric
- sturdy tape
- scissors
- markers, crayons or paint with brushes
- large piece of sturdy cardboard
- cardboard cutting tool
- thumb tack
- piece of string, about a half meter long
- dowel or rod
- colored paper, glue (opt.)

Set up table(s) with stepladder on one side. Cut cloth to size of table length and height. Draw mill on fabric with markers, crayons, or paint or use dark fabric. Tape cloth to hang from tabletop to floor, downstage. Use thumb tack to secure one end of the piece of string in the center of the cardboard and, with a marker or crayon tied to the other end of the string, swing an arc from the center, drawing a circle on the cardboard. Take out the tack and string and cut out the circle. Cut a small hole in the center, just large enough for the dowel to go through. Draw or paint watermill or windmill designs on cardboard, or decorate with colored paper. Cut a slit in the cloth for the muileann actor to stick her head through, or the actor could possible perch behind the mill wheel. Securely tape the dowel on one end of the tabletop, from upstage to downstage, protruding over the end of the table a few centimeters. Slide the mill wheel through the dowel so that it can spin freely. Create a "nut" out of tape and cardboard at the end of the dowel to keep the wheel from falling off.

STONES

• 2 very large paper bags	• newspaper or other paper stuffing
• stapler	• black or gray paint
• paint brushes	• overhead pipe (opt.)
• strong string or yarn (opt.)	• tape (opt.)

Stuff the bags with paper, staple closed to create a roughly spherical shape, and paint. During the magic scenes, the stones can be simply set in place. If you have something like an overhead pipe over the mill area, tie a long string to each stone and, with a weight tied to the other end of the string, throw the string over the pipe so that you can raise and lower the stones onto the mill set. The ends of the strings can be taped down somewhere, such that the actors can easily lift up the tape and move the strings. Use two different colors of string for the two stones, so that the actors know which is for which stone.

LANDSCAPE BACKDROP
- heavy butcher paper
- markers, crayons or paint with brushes
- sturdy tape
- scissors

Cut the butcher paper to fit across upstage wall. Draw scenes of the Irish countryside with markers, crayons, or paint. Make sure the artists understand which end is up and that drawings must be large enough to be seen from audience. Tape to wall.

APPENDIX C: PROPS

PROPS LIST

Long Leather Bag (may have gold and silver props in it)
3 Bannocks (round, flat loaves of bread)
3 Traveling Bags
Broom
White Rod
Shearing Tool
Milk Pail
Tether(s)

APPENDIX D: COSTUMES

COSTUME LIST

MATHAIR & DAUGHTERS: poor peasant clothes
CAILLEACH: dark, witchlike clothing
ALL ANIMALS: plain pants & shirt, or leotard & tights with construction paper ears and cloth tails
MUILLEAN: all black clothes and may wear face paint

HOW TO MAKE THE COSTUMES

ANIMAL EARS
- colored construction paper
- pencil
- scissors
- stapler
- ruler
- light cardboard, glue (optional)
- markers, crayons, paint with brushes, (optional)
- fake fur, glue (optional)

Draw and cut out shape of animal ears with pencil on appropriate color of paper. Cut long strips of the same colors, approximately 4 cm wide and long enough to go around the actors' heads with a 2-3 centimeters of overlap. Staple ears to strips, and staple strips to fit snugly around the actors' heads. You may want to reinforce ears and strips with a cardboard backing. Decorate as needed with markers, crayons, paint, or bits of fake fur.

ANIMAL TAILS
- long strips, approx. 1 meter long, of colored chiffon or other light fabric
- scissors
- long, elastic strip or safety pins

Measure out three strips of fabric. Braid together and tie in a knot at either end. Tail is either pinned to back of actor's pants or tied to an elastic strip that is measured and tied to fit around actor's waist. The best place to pin the tail to pants is through belt loops. If you pin it directly to pants or shirt, it can rip the fabric if someone steps on the tail.

APPENDIX E: SOUND & MUSIC

SOUND:
Magic of Cailleach changing the Daughters into stone: chimes, percussion instruments, and so forth

MUSIC:
"dTigeas A Damhsa" (included) or other Irish folksong
Irish music to play during scene changes, live or on tape or CD

dTIGEAS A DAMHSA
("Come Dance")

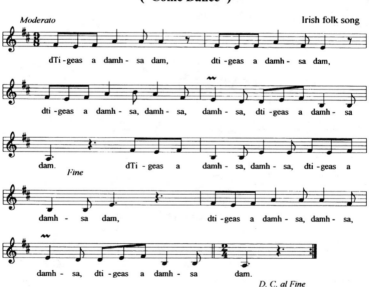

LOS MARIACHIS MEXICANOS
"The Brementown Musicians"
(Mexico)

This play is a good one to do when you have a limited amount of rehearsal time because the story is familiar, the lines are repetitious, and the Narrator's directions make it easy for the actors to know what to do next. It can also be done with a large cast, as long as the chase scenes are carefully blocked and you have a large enough stage area.

"The Brementown Musicians" is an old, classic tale which should be included in every child's literature education, and this setting in Mexico makes this play a good Spanish language activity. It's also great for both music and movement education.

This script has two high-energy attack and chase scenes which are really fun for the kids. Carefully plan out the blocking for these scenes and rehearse them in slow motion. Teach your cast that when actors dramatize "chaos," in reality they are carefully controlling their movements.

There's potential for creative use of your performance space with this play. In the opening scene, when the animals are traveling along the road, the actors can travel around the entire performance space, such as around the perimeters of the audience. Take it one step farther and have the audience walk with the actors along an interesting route where they meet up with the various characters along the way. For example, the audience could follow the actors out into a hallway, into another room, outside, and then back to the theater where they can sit down for the remaining of the play.

The animal roles can all be played as small groups of characters to accomodate a large cast (for example, "Burro" can become "Los Burros"). For simplicity, these roles are written as singular in the script—see Appendix A for plural forms of these Spanish words.

RUNNING TIME OF SHOW: *(approximate)*
    15 minutes
REHEARSAL TIME NEEDED:
    6-8 hours
OTHER PRODUCTION TIME NEEDED:
    3-4 hours
CAST SIZE:
    Minimum: 6, plus Narrator (Patron can be played by an actor who plays Animal or Bandido and you can have only 2 Bandidos.)
    Maximum: 25-30
GENDER OF CHARACTERS:
    All roles can be played by either girls or boys. Note the differences between feminine and masculine forms in the Spanish vocabulary list, Appendix A.

CHARACTERS:
    NARRATOR
    PATRÓN (or PATRONA) – Burro's master
    BURRO – donkey
    GATO (or GATA) – cat
    PERRO – dog
    GALLO (or GALLINA) – Rooster (or Chicken)
    LOS BANDIDOS – the bandits

SCENE 1

(Setting: A small farm in Mexico. No set is needed, but there may be a backdrop of a rural landscape. GATA, PERRO, and GALLO are backstage, each in a different area of the stage or other areas of the performance space, such as around the perimeters of the audience. GALLO will need to have some sort of perch. LIGHTS UP.)

NARRATOR: There was once *un burro* who lived in *México*, in Mexico.

(BURRO enters.)

NARRATOR: *Burro* was getting old. One day he heard his *patrón*, his master, say:

(PATRÓN enters.)

PATRÓN: That *burro* is getting too old to work! So why should I feed him?

(PATRÓN exits.)

BURRO: If *mi patrón* won't feed me, I'll run away! I will go to *Ciudad de México*, Mexico City, and join *un mariachi* band!

NARRATOR: *Burro* set off down the road to *Ciudad de México*. As he went, he sang this song:

BURRO: *(Singing:)*
Soy un Mariachi,
Yo vivo en México!
Everybody loves it when
Yo canto en español!
Hee, haw! Hee, haw! (and so on)

(As BURRO sings, he travels along the road. PERRO enters and lays on the floor, looking very old and sad.)

NARRATOR: Along the way, *Burro* met *un perro*, a dog.

BURRO: *Hola, Perro!*

PERRO: *(Sadly.) Hola, Burro.*

BURRO: Why do you look so sad?

PERRO: I'm getting too old to hunt and for that *mi patrón* says he's going to kill me! So I ran away. But what should I do now?

BURRO: Come with me to *Ciudad de México!* We'll join *un mariachi* band!

PERRO: *Sí!*

ALL: *(Singing:)*
Soy un mariachi,
Yo vivo en México!
Everybody loves it when
Yo canto en español!
Rruff, rruff! Rruff, rruff! (and so on)

(As they sing, they travel down the road. GATO enters and lays down, looking very old and sad.)

NARRATOR: After awhile they met *un gato,* a cat.

BURRO & PERRO: *Hola, Gato!*

GATO: *(Sadly.) Hola, Burro. Hola, Perro.*

BURRO & PERRO: Why do you look so sad?

GATO: I'm getting too old to run after mice and for that, *mi patrona* says she's going to drown me! So I ran away. But what should I do now?

BURRO & PERRO: Come with us to *Ciudad de México!* We'll join *un mariachi* band!

GATO: *Sí!*

ALL: *(Singing.)*
Soy un mariachi,
Yo vivo en México!
Everybody loves it when
Yo canto en español!
Meow, meow! Meow, meow! (and so on)

(As they sing, they travel down the road. GALLO enters and sits on a fence.)

NARRATOR: After awhile they met *un gallo,* a rooster, sitting on a fence and crowing sadly.

BURRO, PERRO & GATO: *Hola, Gallo!*

GALLO: *Hola, Burro. Hola, Perro. Hola, Gato.*

BURRO, PERRO & GATO: Why do you look so sad?

GALLO: I heard *mi patrona* say she was going to cut off my head and make me into chicken soup! So I ran away. But what should I do now?

BURRO, PERRO & GATO: Come with us to *Ciudad de México!* We'll
    join *un mariachi* band!
GALLO: *Si!*
ALL: *(Singing:)*
    Soy un mariachi
    Yo vivo en México!
    Everybody loves it when
    Yo canto en español!
    Cock-a-doodle-doo! (and so on)

    (As they sing they travel down the road and exit. LIGHTS DOWN.
    Change set: Put up the forest and casa sets.)

SCENE 2

    (Setting: The forest and nearby, the casa of LOS BANDIDOS. The
    casa has a large window with a paper windowpane and possibly a slide
    leading into the casa. There is a fireplace, a doorway, a table loaded
    with food and drink, and some chairs set around the table. On or near
    the table is a large chest filled with gold and jewels and there is a lamp,
    either on the table or the floor. Casa lamp is turned on, otherwise the
    stage is dim to indicate night. BURRO, PERRO, GATO & GALLO,
    tired and sleepy, enter the forest area.)

NARRATOR: At night *los amigos*, the friends, came to a forest. It was
    dark and they were very tired and grumpy.
ALL: When are we going to get there? I'm tired! *(Ad lib.)*
PERRO: *(Pointing toward the casa.)* I see a light!
GATO: It must be *un casa*, a house!
GALLO: Let's go!
ALL: *Si!*

    (LOS AMIGOS travel some distance – such as around the audience –
    toward the casa. Meanwhile, BANDIDOS enter and sit at the table,
    eating, drinking, and counting the gold in the chest. LIGHTS UP.
    LOS AMIGOS come to the casa and pantomine looking through the
    windows.)

BURRO: I see a table full of good things to eat!
PERRO: I see *bandidos*, bandits, at the table!
GATO: They're counting all the *oro*, all the gold they've stolen!

GALLO: And they're singing the counting song!
BANDIDOS: *(Singing:)*
> *Uno, dos, tres,*
> *cuatro, cinco, seis,*
> *siete, ocho, nueve,*
> I can count to *diez!*

NARRATOR: *Los Bandidos* were so stupid they couldn't count higher than ten, *diez*. So whenever they got to *diez*, they started counting all over again.

(BANDIDOS repeat song.)

NARRATOR: *Los Amigos* were very hungry after their long journey and they looked longingly at the food on the table.
PERRO: I'd sure like some of that food!
ALL: *Sí!*
GATO: How can we get rid of *Los Bandidos?*
BURRO: I have a plan!
NARRATOR: *Los Amigos* huddled together to discuss their plan.

(They do so.)

NARRATOR: Soon they were ready.

(They gather around the paper window.)

ALL: *Uno, dos, tres...*

(They crash through the window and run around the casa, chasing LOS BANDIDOS. SOUND EFFECTS: Cymbal or other sounds. LIGHTS may flicker.)

ALL: Hee, haw! Rruff, rruff! Meow, meow! Cock-a-doodle-doo! (and so on)
BANDIDOS: *¡Ay, socorro!!! ¡Ay, socorro!!!* Help! Help!!!

(BANDIDOS flee in terror and hide in the forest. ANIMALES sit at the table, eating, drinking, and counting the oro.)

NARRATOR: After that, *Los Amigos* ate and ate, and enjoyed counting all the *oro* in the treasure chest.
When it got very late, they put out the lights and went to sleep: *Gato* slept by the fireplace, *Perro* curled up inside by the front door,

Burro lay down outside in the yard, and *Gallo* perched on the rooftop.

(They do so, turning out the lamp and going to sleep. LIGHTS DOWN on casa.)

NARRATOR: Meanwhile, *Los Bandidos* were hiding in the forest. One of them asked:

BANDIDO #1: Why did we run away?

BANDIDO #2: There's nothing to be afraid of!

BANDIDO #3: *(Obviously terrified.)* I'm not afraid!

BANDIDO #4: Then let's go back to *la casa* and see what happened!

ALL: *Sí!*

(Trembling with fear, BANDIDOS return to the casa and tiptoe inside. ANIMALES watch them but do not move.)

NARRATOR: *Los Bandidos* went up to the fireplace where *Gato's* eyes were shining in the dark.

BANDIDO #1: Ah! I see there's still some coals burning in the fireplace! I'll use them to light the candle!

(BANDIDO leans over GATO who suddenly jumps up, spitting and scratching. LIGHTS may flicker.)

BANDIDOS: *¡Ay, socorro!!! ¡Ay!, socorro!!!*

(BANDIDOS run out the front door. PERRO jumps up, barking and biting them. As they run into the yard BURRO jumps up, braying and kicking his hind legs at them. Meanwhile, Gallo screams from the rooftop.)

BANDIDOS: *¡Ay, socorro!!! ¡Ay, socorro!!!*

(They run into the forest. ANIMALES stop their noises and settle down again.)

NARRATOR: *Los Bandidos* told each other what happened:

BANDIDO #1: A horrible witch spit at us and scratched us with her sharp nails!

BANDIDO #2: Then a monster near the door stabbed us with a knife!

BANDIDO #3: Then a giant hit us with a club!

BANDIDO #4: And a ghost screamed!

ALL: *¡Ay, socorro!!! ¡Ay, socorro!!!*

(They exit, running.)

NARRATOR: *Los Bandidos* never went back to that *casa* again. But *Burro, Perro, Gato y Gallo* liked *la casa* so much, they stayed there forever.

GALLO: You know, we never did go to *Ciudad de México* and join *un mariachi* band!

ALL: *(Singing:)*
Soy un mariachi,
Yo vivo en México!
Everybody loves it when
Yo canto en español!
Hee, haw! Rruff, rruff! Meow, meow! Cock-a-doodle-doo!

ALL: *¡El fin!* The end!

(LIGHTS DOWN.)

APPENDIX A: VOCABULARY LIST
OF FOREIGN LANGUAGE

SPANISH	ENGLISH	PRONUNCIATION
¡Ay, socorro!	Help!	eye! suh-ko'-ro! *
burro	donkey	boo'-ro *
Ciudad de México	Mexico City	see'-yoo-dahd duh meh'-hee-ko
el fin	the end	el feen'
gallo / gallina	rooster / chicken	gah'-djo / gah-djee'-nah
gato / gata	cat (masc. / fem.)	gah'-toe / gah'-tah
hola	hello	o'-lah
la casa	the house	lah cah'-suh
los amigos	the friends	lohs uh-mee'-gohs
los bandidos	the bandits	lohs bahn-dee'-tohs
mariachi band	a Mexican, musical, street band	mah-ree-ah'-chee bahnd
oro	gold	h'-ro
patrón / patrona	master / mistress	pah-trone' / pah-trone'-ah

| perro | dog | pair'-ro * |
| y | and | ee |

"Soy Un Mariachi" (song):

Soy un mariachi	I am called a mariachi	soy oon mah-ree-ah'-chee
Yo vivo en México	I live in Mexico	yo bee'-bo ahn meh'-hee-ko
Yo canto en español	I sing in Spanish	yo kahn'-to on es-pah-nyohl'

"Uno, Dos, Tres" (song):

uno, dos, tres	1, 2, 3	oo'-no, dohs, trayse
cuatro, cinco, seis	4, 5, 6	kwah'-tro, sink'-o, sayse
siete, ocho, nueve,	7, 8, 9,	see-eh'-tay, o'-cho, new-eh'-vay
diez	10	dee'-ehs

* *NOTE: roll the "r's"*
Plurals: To make the character names plural, add an "s" on the end. The article can be "los" ("the"- plural form, masculine), "las" ("the" – plural form, feminine) or the number of the actors, such as "dos burros" (2 donkeys) or "tres gatos" (3 cats).

APPENDIX B: SETS
SETS LIST

BURRO'S FARM:
    backdrop (optional)

THE ROAD TO CIUDAD DE MÉXICO:
    a fence or other perch for Gallo (table or chair)
    backdrops (optional)

FOREST:
    freestanding wall or backdrop

CASA:
    1 table
    several chairs
    fireplace (freestanding wall or backdrop)
    doorway (indicated by a mat on the floor or 2 chairs)
    window:
        paper window pane
        2 heavy chairs or 2 tall, freestanding poles (for window frame)
        slide (optional)
        table (optional)
        chairs or bench (optional, for access to tabletop)

HOW TO MAKE THE SETS

BACKDROPS (for farm scenes, forest, and casa interior)
- heavy butcher paper
- markers, crayons or paint with brushes
- sturdy tape
- scissors

Cut the paper to fit the wall. With markers, crayons, or paint, draw landscapes, forest or casa interior. Make sure the artists understand which end is up and that their drawings must be large enough to be seen from the audience.

FREESTANDING WALLS (for farm scenes, forest, casa interior)
- very large cardboard box
- scissors
- tape or glue
- markers, crayons or paint with brushes
- colored paper or fabric (optional)
- cardboard cutting knife
- heavy butcher paper

Cut box to create a freestanding wall with accordion folds. Cut two pieces of butcher paper to size of the wall. Tape or glue paper to one or both sides of the wall as needed (if cardboard is plain white, you can eliminate this step). Draw picture of the set on the wall with markers, crayons or paint. Colored paper or fabric can also be used to decorate the wall, using glue or tape.

WINDOW
- butcher paper
- scissors
- 2 heavy chairs OR 2 tall, freestanding poles
   (such as volleyball net poles or microphone stands)
- slide (optional)
- table, with chairs or bench access (optional)
- yardstick or meter stick, pencil
- sturdy tape

Cut paper in a square or rectangle to fit between the two chairs or poles and large enough for the actors to crash through. Using the yardstick, measure and draw horizontal and vertical lines to create several small squares. Cut out the inner squares, the "panes," leaving the cross-frames intact. Tape the window between the two chairs or poles. If using a tabletop and slide, set up the poles on either side of the table and arrange chairs or bench so that the actors can easily climb up to the window and slide into the casa. Make a few spare window panes for rehearsals.

APPENDIX C: PROPS
PROPS LIST

Food & Drink Items (bottles, cups, and so on)
Treasure Chest, Full of Gold, Junk Jewelry, and so on
Lamp

COSTUMES LIST

ANIMALS: plain clothes (pants & shirt or leotard & tights) with construction paper ears, feathers and/or cloth tails

BANDIDOS: pants & shirt. May add on hats, bandannas, eye-patches, beards or mustaches, and ugly scars

BURRO'S PATRON: farm clothes

HOW TO MAKE THE COSTUMES

ANIMAL EARS
- colored construction paper
- pencil
- scissors
- stapler
- light cardboard, glue (optional)
- markers, crayons, paint with brushes, (optional)
- fake fur, glue (optional)

Draw and cut out shape of animal ears with pencil on appropriate color of paper. Cut long strips of the same colors, approximately 4 cm wide and long enough to go around the actors' heads with a 2-3 centimeters of overlap. Staple ears to strips, and staple strips to fit snugly around the actors' heads. You may want to reinforce ears and strips with a cardboard backing. Decorate as needed with markers, crayons, paint, or bits of fake fur.

ANIMAL TAILS
- long strips, approximately 1 meter long, of colored chiffon or other light fabric
- scissors
- long, elastic strip or safety pins

Measure out three strips of fabric. Braid together and tie in a knot at either end. Tail is either pinned to back of actor's pants or tied to an elastic strip that is measured and tied to fit around actor's waist. The best place to pin the tail to pants is through belt loops. If you pin it directly to pants or shirt, it can rip the fabric if someone steps on the tail.

Tail for Gallo:
- feathers (real or made out of paper)
- tape
- long, elastic strip
- string
- scissors

Measure and tie the elastic to fit around the actor's waist. Cut string into several pieces, each approx. 30 cm long. Attach feathers all along the string pieces by wrapping a piece of tape around each feather stem and them wrapping it securely around the string. Tie the string pieces to the elastic waistband. You can also do a similar thing around the actor's head.

SOUND:
    Crashing through the window: cymbals or other noise makers

MUSIC:
    Song: *"Soy Un Mariachi"* (included)
    Song: *"Uno, Dos, Tres"* (included)
    Mexican music to play during scene change, played live or on tape or CD

SOY UN MARIACHI
("I Am A Mariachi Musician")

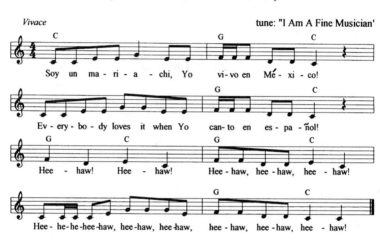

UNO, DOS, TRES
("One, Two, Three")

MA LIEN AND THE MAGIC PAINTBRUSH
(China)

Here is a story of a child who is granted a special power: Everything she paints with the magic paintbrush becomes real. Ma Lien respects the power of the paintbrush and only does good deeds with it. She is captured twice by the evil Mandarin and both times, she cleverly outwits him. It's a wonderful fantasy and the special effects of the pictures coming to life are worth the effort to create them. There's also a couple of fun chase-and-capture scenes.

Some Chinese Mandarin language and a song are included. The Latin alphabet spellings in this script are based on the Mainland China system for Latin spellings. Taiwan and Hong Kong have different systems for spelling Chinese with the Latin alphabet, the alphabet we use for the English language.

RUNNING TIME OF SHOW: *(approximate)*
 20-25 minutes
REHEARSAL TIME NEEDED:
 10-12 hours
OTHER PRODUCTION TIME NEEDED:
 4-5 hours
CAST SIZE:
 Minimum: 8, plus Narrator (There can be a minimum of 2 Wèi-Bing and 2 Peasants & Prisoners, the Wèi-Bing can double as Rooster and Water Buffalo, and Hwà-ja and Shén-xian can double as Peasants, Prisoners or Horses.)
 Maximum: 25-30 (There can be numerous Wèi-Bing, Peasants, Prisoners and Horses and the Paintbrush can be played by an actor.)
GENDER OF CHARACTERS:
 All the major characters are traditionally portrayed as male, but can be played as either male or female.

CHARACTERS:
 NARRATOR
 MA LIEN – a poor Chinese girl or boy
 MANDARIN – a greedy public official
 HWÀ-JA – a famous painter
 SHÉN-XIAN – a wizard
 WÈI-BING – guards of the Mandarin
 PEASANTS & PRISONERS
 ROOSTER
 WATER BUFFALO
 HORSES
 MAGIC PAINTBRUSH (optional)

SCENE 1

(Setting: A rural area of pre-Revolutionary China. There may be a landscape backdrop. In one area of the stage is the HWÀ-JA'S house. There is an easel with a portrait of the MANDARIN on it and nearby are paint and brushes. There may be an interior wall or other set that includes a window for MA LIEN to peek through. In another area of the stage is MA LIEN'S peasant hut. There is an interior wall on which are charcoal drawings and a piece of charcoal – may use a crayon or marker – lies nearby. There may be some type of set which allows ROOSTER to magically come to life from a drawing – see Appendix B for ideas. LIGHTS UP.)

NARRATOR: In China there once lived a poor peasant child named Ma Lien.

(MA LIEN enters.)

NARRATOR: Ma Lien was a very talented artist, but she was so poor she had no money with which to buy a paintbrush.
One day, as Ma Lien trudged home after a long day of working in the fields, she passed by the house of a famous painter, the *Hwà-ja*.

(HWÀ-JA and MANDARIN enter HWÀ-JA'S house. HWÀ-JA paints at the easel while MANDARIN poses. MA LIEN looks through the window at them.)

NARRATOR: Ma Lien peeked into the window and watched the *Hwà-Ja* work. She was painting a portrait of the Mandarin, the rich public official of Ma Lien's district.

MANDARIN: Be sure to make me look very handsome!

HWÀ-JA: Yes, my lord.

MA LIEN: *(Speaking through the window.)* Oh, great *Hwà-Ja!* Please, may I have one of your old brushes, one you don't need anymore?

HWÀ-JA: *BÙ!* NO! Get out of here!

(HWÀ-JA chases MA LIEN away. HWÀ-JA and MANDARIN exit. MA LIEN goes to another area of the stage and pantomimes the following.)

NARRATOR: But Ma Lien would not be discouraged. She drew pictures wherever she could, using a stone to scratch on a flat rock, or with her fingers in the wet sand of the riverbank.

When she went back to her hut at night, she drew pictures on the wall with a piece of charcoal.

(MA LIEN goes to hut and draws on her wall. May pantomine.)

NARRATOR: One night, Ma Lien looked around her room at all the pictures and sighed.

MA LIEN: If only I had a brush, what beautiful pictures I would paint!

(SOUND & LIGHT EFFECTS: SHÉN-XIAN magically appears, with paintbrush. Paintbrush can be either a prop or played by an actor.)

SHÉN-XIAN: *Ni-hao,* Ma Lien!

MA LIEN: *Ni-hao, Shén-Xian!*

SHÉN-XIAN: Ma Lien, you have worked very hard and now you have earned a paintbrush. Use it wisely for it has great power!

(SHÉN-XIAN gives the brush to MA LIEN.)

MA LIEN: *Xìe-xìe!* Thank you!

SHÉN-XIAN: *Zài-jiàn!*

MA LIEN: *Zài-jiàn!*

(SOUND & LIGHT EFFECTS: SHÉN-XIAN magically disappears. MA LIEN goes over to the wall and draws a rooster. SOUND & LIGHT EFFECTS: ROOSTER comes to life. This can be done with either a special effects set or the ROOSTER can simply appear from behind the hut wall. ROOSTER flies around the hut.)

ROOSTER: COCK-A-DOODLE-DOO!!!

(ROOSTER exits.)

MA LIEN: Now I know why the *Shén-Xian* said this brush has great power! I *will* use it wisely!

(LIGHTS DOWN. Change set: Remove HWÀ-JA'S house and MA LIEN'S hut and set up MANDARIN'S palace and boulder.)

SCENE 2

(Setting: MANDARIN'S palace and nearby rice paddy. The MAN-DARIN'S palace has a thronelike chair and may include an interior

wall. There is either a wall or easels for the two drawings for Scene 4. If using easels, they can be backstage for the present time. The drawing of the tree of gold is already made and covered with a cloth that can be easily removed. The mountain of gold will be drawn during Scene 4 and so a large piece of blank paper is already taped on the wall or an easel. In another area of the palace is the dungeon with a freestanding interior wall that can be easily knocked over. Backstage are the sea and ship props for Scene 4. In another area of the stage is the rice paddy. The only set needed is a large boulder, made of a table or chairs covered with a cloth, underneath which the WATER BUFFALO is hidden. LIGHTS UP.)

NARRATOR: The next morning, as she was walking to the fields to work, Ma Lien passed a rice paddy. There she saw some peasants pulling a heavy plow.

(MA LIEN enters, with paintbrush. PEASANTS enter pulling a long rope, pantomiming pulling a heavy plow. The other end of the rope is tied in a loop large enough to slip around WATER BUFFALO's waist.)

MA LIEN: *Ni-hao!*
PEASANTS: *Ni-hao!*
NARRATOR: Ma Lien went over to a large boulder and painted a strong and healthy water buffalo.

(MA LIEN "paints" on boulder – actor should stand upstage of boulder so that the audience does not see the pantomimed "painting." MANDARIN and WÈI-BING enter and watch from a distance. SOUND & LIGHT EFFECTS as WATER BUFFALO magically comes charging out from the boulder. The PEASANTS chase after it and capture it.)

PEASANT #1: Just what we need to pull our plow!
PEASANT #2: *Xìe-xìe*, Ma Lien!

(PEASANTS slip one end of the rope around WATER BUFFALO'S waist and they plow the paddy more easily now.)

NARRATOR: The Mandarin happened upon this scene and witnessed the power of Ma Lien's paintbrush. He wanted this power for himself.
MANDARIN: Seize her!!

(WÈI-BING chase and capture MA LIEN. May include SOUND EFFECTS: Drums, gong or other sounds. They take her to the palace. PEASANTS and WATER BUFFALO exit. PRISONERS enter and sit in dungeon.)

MANDARIN: Throw her in the dungeon!

(WÈI-BING throw her in the dungeon, lock the door, and exit. Some WÈI-BING remain outside the door to guard it. MANDARIN sits on his throne.)

NARRATOR: Ma Lien could see that the other prisoners were suffering and she spoke kindly to them.

MA LIEN: Why are you here?

PRISONER #2: The Mandarin imprisoned us so he could steal our lands!

PRISONER #1: We haven't done anything wrong!

(LIGHTS DIM to indicate night. WÈI-BING and MANDARIN fall asleep.)

NARRATOR: When it was night, Ma Lien waited until the Wèi-Bing dozed off. Then quickly, she painted a door on the wall. She also painted some fine horses.

(MA LIEN "paints" a door on the dungeon wall – pantomime – and it magically opens: Actors merely push the free-standing wall over. HORSES enter and MA LIEN and PRISONERS quietly lead them out of the palace, past the sleeping WÈI-BING, then "mount" the HORSES and take off. HORSE actors can be on their hands and knees or can run on two feet. If the latter, their "riders" either place their hands on the HORSES' shoulders or hold a rope that is loosely tied around the HORSES' chests or waists. The WÈI-BING wake up and, with much shouting, chase them. MA LIEN, PRISONERS, and HORSES escape and exit. WÈI-BING go to the MANDARIN.)

WÈI-BING #1: Mandarin! Wake up! Ma Lien and the other prisoners have escaped!

MANDARIN: Why did you let this happen, fools?!!

WÈI-BING: #2: It was the magic paintbrush!

WÈI-BING #3: Ma Lien painted a door in the dungeon wall!

MANDARIN: I will have you killed for this! Go find Ma Lien! Seize
her and bring her to me!

WÈI-BING #4: Can't we wait until morning?

MANDARIN: *Bù!* Now!!

(WÈI-BING exit. MANDARIN exits. LIGHTS DOWN.)

SCENE 3

(Setting: The same, a few months later. LIGHTS UP.)

NARRATOR: Ma Lien knew that she would not be safe if she
remained on the Mandarin's lands, so she rode for many miles to
villages far from her home. There she continued to help anyone she
could with her magic paintbrush, painting work animals and food
for the poor peasants, and toys for their children.

*(The following Narration is optional, to be used to introduce song if it
is included in the production.)*

NARRATOR: Ma Lien ended up in a village high in the mountains,
where all the people worked as rock cutters in a big stone quarry.

*(MA LIEN & PEASANTS enter and get into position for song.
MUSIC BEGINS: "Four Powers." Actors may do stong quarrying
movements, such as hammering, to the beat of the song. MUSIC ENDS.)*

(If song is not performed, MA LIEN and PEASANTS enter now.)

NARRATOR: Ma Lien and her wonderful paintbrush soon became
known throughout the land. Eventually the Mandarin learned
where Ma Lien was living.

*(WÈI-BING enter, chase MA LIEN and capture her. SOUND
EFFECTS: Drums, gong, or other sound. They take her back to the
palace as MANDARIN enters.)*

MANDARIN: *Ni-hao,* Ma Lien!

(MA LIEN is silent. MANDARIN grabs the paintbrush.)

MANDARIN: I don't think you'll escape so easily without your paintbrush! *Wei-bing!* Throw Ma Lien in the dungeon!

(WÈI-BING throw her in the dungeon, lock the door, and return to the MANDARIN.)

MANDARIN: Now go get the *Hwà-ja* and bring her to me!

(WÈI-BING exit and return with HWÀ-JA, who bows before the MANDARIN.)

MANDARIN: *Ni-hao, Hwà-Ja.*
HWÀ-JA: *Ni-hao,* my lord.
MANDARIN: Paint me a tree with leaves of gold that will fall like rain when I shake the branches!

(HWÀ-JA "paints" – pantomime – a tree of gold on the wall or an easel which is now brought onstage. The drawing is already made and covered with a cloth which is now removed.)

MANDARIN: GOLD!!!

(He rushes at the picture, bumps his head on it, and falls down.)

MANDARIN: AAAHHH!!! It's not real! I will have you killed for this!
HWÀ-JA: *(Terrified.)* Only Ma Lien can make the magic work!
MANDARIN: *WÈI-BING!* Bring Ma Lien to me!

(WÈI-BING run to the dungeon, get MA LIEN and bring her to the MANDARIN.)

MANDARIN: Ma Lien, if you will paint but one picture for me, I will give you your freedom!
MA LIEN: *(Thinks a moment.)* Okay.
MANDARIN: *Hwà-Ja!* Give Ma Lien the paintbrush!

(HWÀ-JA does so.)

MANDARIN: Paint me a mountain of pure gold!

(MA LIEN draws a sea. The drawing will be made during the scene with the markers that are incorporated into either the paintbrush prop or, if played by an actor, into the paintbrush actor's costume. A long, blue cloth is brought out and held across stage by actors at both ends who, gently at first, wave the cloth up and down.)

MANDARIN: Why do you paint the sea? I ordered a mountain of gold!

MA LIEN: I'm not finished.

(MA LIEN draws a large, gold mountain rising out of the sea.)

MANDARIN: Beautiful! Beautiful! Now paint me a ship so I can sail to my mountain!

(MA LIEN draws a ship on the sea. The ship – a large, decorated cardboard box is brought onstage. MANDARIN and WÈI-BING crowd into it.)

MANDARIN: Too slow! Too slow! Paint me a wind to speed us along!

(SOUND & LIGHT EFFECTS: MA LIEN draws a wind which makes the waves rise about the ship. She paints storm clouds and EFFECTS increase. The ship tosses about on the water. The storm increases in intensity as MA LIEN draws more of the storm and all aboard the ship cry out frantically. The ship falls over and the MAN-DARIN and WÈI-BING fall overboard and frantically try to swim. Eventually they either "drown" – lay down under the blue cloth – or make it to shore and run away. The storm dies down. SOUND & LIGHT EFFECTS STOP.)

NARRATOR: After that, Ma Lien returned to her simple life with the peasants, always ready to help them with their work. And never again was Ma Lien forced to use her magic paintbrush for evil and greed.

ALL: *Wén-le!* The end!

APPENDIX A: VOCABULARY LIST
OF FOREIGN LANGUAGE

CHINESE (spelled with Latin alphabet)	ENGLISH	PRONUNCIATION
bù	no	boo
zài-jiàn	good-bye	d'zi-jyehn'
hwà-ja	painter, artist	hwah'-jyah
ni hao	hello	nee'-how
shén-xian	wizard, magician	shen-sh'yen'
xìe-xìe	thank you	shay'-shay
wán-le	the end	wahn'-luh
wèi-bing	guards	way-bing'

SETS LIST

HWÀ-JA'S HOUSE:
easel
Mandarin's portrait
interior wall with window (optional)

MA LIEN'S HUT:
interior wall, plain with black drawings on it
special effects set for rooster (optional)

BOULDER:
1 table or 2 chairs, covered with a cloth

MANDARIN'S PALACE:
1 thron-like chair
2 easels or a wall
a tree of gold
cloth (to cover tree painting)
large piece of white paper (for mountain of gold drawing)
dungeon wall – light, freestanding
ship
palace interior wall (optional)

LANDSCAPE BACKDROP (optional)

HOW TO MAKE THE SETS

INTERIOR WALLS (for Hwà-Ja's house, Ma Lien's hut, dungeon wall, and
palace interior)
• very large cardboard box
• cardboard cutting knife
• scissors
• heavy butcher paper
• tape or glue
• markers, crayons or paint with brushes
• colored paper or fabric (optional)
Cut box to create a freestanding wall with accordion folds. For Hwà-Ja's house cut
a window for Ma Lien to peek through. Cut a piece of butcher paper to the size of
the wall. Tape or glue paper to the wall (if cardboard is plain white, you can elim-
inate this step). Draw picture of the set on the wall with markers, crayons, or

paint. Colored paper or fabric can also be used to decorate the wall, using glue or tape.

SPECIAL EFFECTS SET FOR ROOSTER
- 2 sturdy, freestanding poles, such as microphone stands or volleyball net poles, or 2 heavy chairs
- large piece of butcher paper
- scissors
- markers, crayons or paint with brushes
- tape
- large piece of cloth

Draw a large rooster on the paper. Cut several little slits in the paper which will make it easier to tear. Suspend and tape the paper between the two poles or chairs. Cover the drawing with the cloth. During the scene, the cloth is pulled off to reveal the drawing while Ma Lien pantomimes drawing it. The Rooster actor then bursts through the paper. Make some extra drawings for rehearsals.

SHIP
- very large cardboard box
- strong tape
- paint
- paint brushes
- Mast: (optional)
  long, thick dowel
  1 or 2 shorter dowels
  fabric pieces
  stapler

Fold and tape open the top of the box. Paint the outside of the box. When dry, it's possible to paint Chinese characters or other designs on the ship. (In lieu of paint, cover the outside of the ship with butcher paper and decorate with markers or crayons.) To make mast, lay the shorter dowels across the longer one and tape securely. Cut sail pieces out of fabric and tape or staple around the dowels to secure. Mast can be handheld by one of the actors in the ship.

LANDSCAPE BACKDROP
- heavy butcher paper
- markers, crayons or paint with brushes
- sturdy tape
- scissors

Cut butcher paper to fit across upstage wall. Draw scenes of the Chinese country-side with markers, crayons, or paint. Make sure the artists understand which end is up and that drawings must be large enough to be seen from the audience. Tape to wall.

PROPS LIST

Paintbrushes, Paints (for Hwà-Ja)
Charcoal (can use black crayon or marker)
Large, Magic Paintbrush (with blue, yellow or gold and black markers
   affixed to it, for the mountain of gold drawing)
Rope (for plow)
Swords (for Wèi-bing, optional)

HOW TO MAKE THE PROPS

WÈI-BING SWORDS
• big Styrofoam or heavy cardboard pieces
• cutting tool
• duct tape

Draw sword shape on Styrofoam or cardboard and cut out. Completely cover with duct tape. If using cardboard, make sure it's very thick as lightweight cardboard will bend easily during rehearsals.

APPENDIX D: COSTUMES

COSTUMES LIST

MA LIEN: poor, peasant clothes
HWÀ-JA and MANDARIN: rich-looking, Chinese robes
SHEN-XIAN: Chinese robes or other, magical outfit
WÈI-BING: plain, matching uniforms, such as tunics, and possibly hats,
   swords
PEASANTS & PRISONERS: poor, peasant clothes
ROOSTER: plain, red clothes with tail feathers
WATER BUFFALO: plain dark clothes, with horns and tail
HORSES: plain clothes with ears and tails
PAINTBRUSH: plain dark or colored clothing and a pocket for carrying
   markers for the mountain of gold drawing. The actor's hair can be gath-
   ered in a ponytail at the top of his/her head.

HOW TO MAKE THE COSTUMES

ROOSTER TAIL FEATHERS
• feathers   • tape

- long, elastic strip   • string
- scissors

Measure and tie the elastic to fit around the actor's waist. Cut string into several pieces, each approx. 30 cm long. Attach feathers all along the string pieces by wrapping a piece of tape around each feather stem and then wrapping it securely around the string. Tie the string pieces to the elastic waistband. You can also do a similar thing around the actor's head.

WATER BUFFALO HORNS

- a small piece of brown, sturdy cardboard
- scissors
- wide, black elastic band, long enough to fit around actor's head
- stapler

Draw horns on the cardboard and cut out. Measure, cut, and staple the elastic to fit around the actor's head. Staple the horns to the elastic.

HORSE EARS

- colored construction paper   • pencil
- scissors   • stapler
- light cardboard, glue (optional)
- markers, crayons, paint with brushes (optional)

Draw and cut out shape of ears with pencil on paper. Cut long strips of the same color, approximately 4 cm wide and long enough to go around the actors' heads with a 2-3 centimeters of overlap. Staple ears to strips, and staple strips to fit snugly around the actors' heads. You may want to reinforce ears and strips with a cardboard backing. Decorate as needed with markers, crayons, or paint.

HORSE & WATER BUFFALO TAILS

- long strips, approximately 1 meter long, of colored chiffon or other light fabric
- scissors
- long, elastic strip or safety pins

Measure out three strips of fabric. Braid together and tie in a knot at either end. Tail is either pinned to back of actor's pants or tied to an elastic strip that is measured and tied to fit around actor's waist. The best place to pin the tail to pants is through belt loops. If you pin it directly to pants or shirt, it can rip the fabric if someone steps on the tail.

APPENDIX E: SOUND & MUSIC

SOUND:

Magic of Shén-Xian's entrance/exit and Rooster and Water Buffalo coming to life: percussion or other instruments

Chase/capture scenes: drums, gong or other percussion instruments

Storm: drums, percussion and other instruments and a large strip of heavy aluminum (shake it to sound like thunder & lightning)

MUSIC:

Song: "Four Powers" (included)

Percussion for song: All actors strike two stones together on the first beat in every measure

Chinese music to play during set change, played live or on tape or CD

FOUR POWERS

Moderato   Pamela Gerke

Wind o-ver moun-tain sings a song, it is a
song of earth; sun thru the rain paints
co-lors bright, it is a rain-bow of sky.
Wind, moun-tain, sun, and rain,
there is much po-wer in each. Air, Earth,
Fi-re, Wa-ter, too, each has great les-sons to
teach. Wind o-ver moun-tain: sing!

STAR STORY
(Lushootseed Salish)

This story comes from the Lushootseed Salish, the Native American, or "First People," of the Puget Sound region of Western Washington, around Seattle. The Lushootseed have a rich oral tradition which has only been made into a written form in the last few decades. *Star Story* is an important story in the Lushootseed tradition and some other versions of it are called *Star Child* and *Diaper Boy.* This version was told by Lucy Williams in 1954.

I was fortunate to have received approval for adapting some Lushootseed tales to play format from Vi Hilbert, translator and editor of much of the Lushootseed oral tradition (see Volume 2 of this series for more Lushootseed plays). All teachers in search of multicultural experiences for their students must be sensitive to the issues around "cultural appropriation," when people of the dominant (white) culture use the traditions of people of other cultures, such as Native Americans, without permission. Always take care to seek education from authentic resources (people, books, and so on) when preparing a play production of a story from another culture.

There are many tribes in the Puget Sound region, each with their own language and traditions. It's a common mistake to lump together many different Native American tribes as if they were all the same. The Lushootseed Salish words and story in this play are specifically from the area north of the present Snohomish–King County line, just north of Seattle.

For this play, I've used as much as possible of the actual language of the English translation from the telling by the storyteller who was the source for this tale in one of Vi Hilbert's books. I've done this in order to retain some of the flavor of the traditional telling of this story and this is why some of the lines may seem to be not grammatically correct.

I've also included a short write-up about Lushootseed Salish culture, in Appendix F. Whereas the other cultures and countries represented in this book can most likely be researched at local libraries, information on Lushootseed Salish culture may prove difficult or impossible to find (even in Seattle).

The number four comes into play several times in this story. This is because four is the traditional number used in stories from this region, just as the number three figures highly in European tales. Like so many old stories, *Star Story* explains the origin of natural resources – the sun and moon, rivers, and lakes.

This is the story of a Young Man's "spirit journey." A "spirit journey" is when a person goes on a journey of self-discovery and comes back with the wisdom of self-knowledge or spiritual insight. Spirit journeys are respected in the culture of the First People and many are recorded as stories.

"Spirit songs" are personal songs which are given to each person by spiritual powers and the singing of a person's own spirit songs brings them strength and energy. The songs included for the Lushootseed stories in this collection reportedly have an origin in Native American songs but have been altered and adapted over many years and many campfires.

RUNNING TIME OF SHOW: *(approximate)*
    25-30 minutes
REHEARSAL TIME NEEDED:
    10-12 hours
OTHER PRODUCTION TIME NEEDED:
    3-4 hours
CAST SIZE:
    Minimum: 10, plus Narrator (Younger Sister, White Star, and Blue Star can play other roles; Log People can also play Daylight Girls and all the characters in the last scene.)
    Maximum: 25-30 (Can add additional Lushootseed Elders and other People.)

GENDER OF CHARACTERS:
    Log People, Elk, Raven, Elders, and Lushootseed people can be played as either female or male; all others should be played as described.

CHARACTERS:

NARRATOR

ELDER SISTER – mother of Star Boy

YOUNGER SISTER

WHITE STAR – husband of Elder Sister

BLUE STAR – husband of Younger Sister

LOG PEOPLE (3)

GRANDMOTHER LOG – Star Boy's baby-sitter

STAR BOY

DAYLIGHT GIRLS (4)

PIPICIK

ELK

RAVEN

MOLE

MAGPIE

MOUSE

FROG – Star Boy's bride

GRANDMOTHER FROG

ELDERS (optional)

LUSHOOTSEED PEOPLE (optional)

SCENE 1

(Setting: Earth and Sky. On the back wall is a backdrop of the sky. Two large, sturdy tables are placed upstage. They are at a slight angle to each other so that there is a space between them, large enough for the actors to fit through. Blue cloth hangs from the table tops to the floor, downstage, decorated as the sky. Nearby is a rope, pre-tied with a slip-knot to easily go around ELDER SISTER'S waist. There are some paper ferns taped on the hanging cloth, near the space between the tables. On the floor is a river, represented by a long, blue cloth which is laid across the stage, and there may be trees or bushes. On one side of the stage is RAVEN'S house, made of a table and two freestanding walls on either side of it and a light, cardboard piece laid across the edge of the table and the upstage section of the walls, making a roof which is easily removed. Nearby is a canoe – a decorated child's wagon – and there may be a broom. On the other side of the stage is a space for ELDER SISTER'S campsite and a campfire set is backstage. BLUE STAR & WHITE STAR enter carrying bows and arrows and stand on tabletops. LIGHTS UP.)

NARRATOR: This is a story told by the Lushootseed Salish, the first people of the Puget Sound region in what is now Washington State. One day, two young sisters were getting some fern roots to dry.

(SISTERS enter, with gathering baskets.)

NARRATOR: They walked far to look for better roots. When they camped, they lay down and looked at the sky.

(SISTERS do so, on the floor.)

YOUNGER SISTER: I wish that Blue Star was my husband!
ELDER SISTER: I wish that White Star was my husband!

(They go to sleep. STARS come down from sky and take the SISTERS, sleepwalking, up to the sky. The SISTERS wake up and ELDER SISTER looks with horror at WHITE STAR.)

ELDER SISTER: Oh! You are ugly!
WHITE STAR: It was your idea to marry me!
NARRATOR: Oh, that older girl felt bad. She thought it was a pretty star when she first saw it. Well, the two Star Brothers went hunting. Before they left they told the sisters:

STARS: Don't dig those fern roots that go straight down!

(STARS go to another part of the stage.)

NARRATOR: The men went for four days. On the fourth day the Older Sister decided to dig the roots that go straight down.

(SISTER pantomime digging at space between two tables, by the ferns.)

NARRATOR: They dug more and more, and pretty soon they got a hole.

(SOUND EFFECT: WIND. SISTERS peer down the "hole.")

NARRATOR: A lot of wind came out of that hole. The Star husbands were out hunting and felt that wind and thought:

STARS: There's a hole to the next world! They found out!!

NARRATOR: The Older Sister wanted to go back home. They made a long rope of little cedar trees, called *huh-pai'*, braided together.

(SISTERS pull out rope, pantomime braiding it together.)

NARRATOR: Elder Sister had a baby in her belly, so her sister helped her tie the rope around her waist.

(YOUNGER SISTER ties rope around ELDER SISTER'S waist and then holds on to one end as ELDER SISTER goes through hole down to the ground.)

NARRATOR: When Elder Sister got to the ground, she pulled the rope four times to let her sister know she'd made it all right.

(ELDER SISTER pulls the rope four times, unties it from her waist, and exits. YOUNGER SISTER pulls up the rope and exits. LIGHTS DOWN.)

SCENE 2

(Setting: The same, a few months later. GRANDMOTHER LOG & LOG PEOPLE enter and lie down on the floor. Backstage, ELDER SISTER stuffs a pillow in her shirt to make herself look pregnant. LIGHTS UP.)

NARRATOR: Now the Elder Sister walked and looked around to make a home.

(ELDER SISTER enters.)

NARRATOR: She was close to the time when her baby would be born. She wanted a *kai'-yah*, a grandmother, to take care of her baby when she would be out getting food. She looked around and saw rotten logs. She kicked one log four times and it turned into a human.

(ELDER SISTER "kicks" LOG PERSON #1, who stands up.)

LOG PERSON #1: Uh...eep..ook...wha... *(Ad lib trying to talk.)*

NARRATOR: It couldn't talk very well, so she kicked it again and it turned back into wood.

(She does so. LOG PERSON lies down again.)

NARRATOR: She tried it again with other rotten logs.

(Repeat the same procedure as above with other TWO LOG PEOPLE.)

NARRATOR: She still wasn't satisfied but when she kicked the fourth log it looked exactly the way *a kai'-yah* should look, a very nice old lady.

(ELDER SISTER "kicks" GRANDMOTHER LOG and she stands up.)

GRANDMOTHER LOG: *Tsi siab!* Hello!
ELDER SISTER: *Tsi siab, kai'-yah!*

(They exit. LIGHTS DOWN. LOG PEOPLE exit.)

SCENE 3

(Setting: The same, a few months later. PIPICIK lies down under the river cloth. LIGHTS UP.)

NARRATOR: A pretty little boy like a little star was born after she got a *kai'-yah*.

(ELDER SISTER enters with "baby" – a doll – in a cradleboard. GRANDMOTHER LOG enters and ELDER SISTER gives her the cradleboard.)

ELDER SISTER: Don't call him a boy or he'll get kidnapped!
GRANDMOTHER LOG: *Aiii.*

(ELDER SISTER begins to exit. SOUND EFFECT: BABY'S CRY.)

GRANDMOTHER: *(To baby:)* Hush, my grandson, my grandson...
Oh! Oh! I mean my granddaughter! My granddaughter!

(ELDER SISTER overhears and comes back.)

ELDER SISTER: *(Angry.)* You crazy, good-for-nothing! Don't call him
a boy or he'll get kidnapped!
GRANDMOTHER LOG: I forgot myself!

(ELDER SISTER exits.)

NARRATOR: Everyday, when the woman went out to collect food, she
told the *kai'-yah* to be sure to not call the baby a boy. On the
fourth day, there were four Daylight Girls walking about who had
no husbands and were looking for a man.

(DAYLIGHT GIRLS enter. SOUND EFFECT: BABY'S CRY.)

GRANDMOTHER LOG: Hush my grandson, my grandson...Oh!
Oh! I mean my granddaughter! My granddaughter!
DAYLIGHT GIRL # 1: She called that baby a boy!
DAYLIGHT GIRL #2: Let's look!

(DAYLIGHT GIRLS look inside the cradleboard.)

DAYLIGHT GIRL #3: It is a boy!
DAYLIGHT GIRL #4: Let's take him away!

*(They take the baby and run away, while GRANDMOTHER tries to
stop them but she cannot run.)*

NARRATOR: The baby's *koi'-yah*, his mother, came back.

(ELDER SISTER enters and sees that the baby is gone.)

ELDER SISTER: Where is the baby?!!
GRANDMOTHER LOG: Some women kidnapped him!
ELDER SISTER: You must have called him a boy!
NARRATOR: She got mad and kicked the old woman and turned her
into wood again.

(She does so and GRANDMOTHER LOG lies down on the floor.)

NARRATOR: The woman didn't know what to do. She wept as she mourned her loss. Pretty soon she took the baby's diaper, made of the soft, inner bark of the *huh-pai'*, the cedar tree, and went to the river to wash her face.

(ELDER SISTER takes diaper, goes to the river and kneels at the bank, pantomiming washing the diaper.)

NARRATOR: She washed the baby's diaper and twisted it four times. It turned into a baby but it wasn't good. She dipped it and twisted it again and it cried.

(She does so. SOUND EFFECT: BABY'S CRY.)

NARRATOR: She dipped and twisted it again and the fourth time it was a fine child.

(She does so. PIPICIK comes out of the river.)

PIPICIK: *Tsi siab, koi'-yah!* Hello, mother!
NARRATOR: His name was Pipicik, which means "Diaper Boy." She built a fire and they lived.

(ELDER SISTER gets campfire set and puts it on one side of the stage. She and PIPICIK sit by it. LIGHTS DOWN. GRANDMOTHER LOG exits.)

SCENE 4

(Setting: RAVEN'S HOUSE and ELDER SISTER'S campsite. RAVEN enters house. All action in his house takes place downstage, in front of the "roof." LIGHTS UP.)

NARRATOR: Upstream, Raven was living in a big house. It was a two-fire size. He is high class, high class.
Suddenly, Raven said:
RAVEN: I'm going by water, by water, by water!
NARRATOR: Raven went downstream.

(RAVEN gets into canoe and paddles down the river toward ELDER SISTER'S campsite.)

142 Star Story

NARRATOR: Then he saw a little smoke and the woman with the child. Raven ran after them and pulled them.

(RAVEN laughs, jumps out of the canoe and grabs ELDER SISTER & PIPICIK. He forces them into the canoe.)

NARRATOR: They were now his slaves. He took his slaves upstream.

(They travel back to RAVEN'S house, get out of the canoe, and go inside. LIGHTS DOWN.)

SCENE 5

(Setting: The Sky. STAR BOY & DAYLIGHT GIRLS enter. STAR BOY carries a bow and arrow and wears a glittery headdress, with stars painted on his face. LIGHTS UP.)

NARRATOR: Meanwhile, the Star Baby grew and was now a great hunter. His face was just like sunshine. He went hunting and the women told him:
DAYLIGHT GIRLS: Don't ever chase elk down that way!

(They point towards earth. STAR BOY moves off to one side, but overhears the following.)

NARRATOR: While he hunted, the Daylight Girls argued with each other:
DAYLIGHT GIRL #1: He's more mine because I found him!
DAYLIGHT GIRL #2: I heard the old lady call him a baby boy!
DAYLIGHT GIRL #3: I examined him and saw he was a boy!
DAYLIGHT GIRL #4: I raised him, too!

(DAYLIGHT GIRLS exit.)

NARRATOR: Now Star Boy knew the truth.
STAR BOY: I was stolen! Now I know why they don't want me to go down that way! I'm going to follow the elk down to there!

(ELK enters and STAR BOY chases her from Sky to Earth. ELK exits. STAR BOY looks around.)

NARRATOR: Pipicik was crying for his brother now, singing a song his *koi'-yah*, his mother had taught him.

(PIPICIK comes out of RAVEN'S house, crying. He gets into the canoe and paddles downstream while singing.)

PIPICIK: *(Singing:)*
Oh woe, oh woe, oh woe,
It is said my brother was stolen away by women
who belonged up river.
I'm from the wringing of my *koi'-yah*.
I've been made a slave by Raven.
STAR BOY: Why are you crying?

(PIPICIK covers his eyes, for he is blinded by STAR BOY'S brightness.)

PIPICIK: My brother was stolen!
STAR BOY: It must be me!
NARRATOR: Pipicik could not see his brother because he was shining too brightly. Star Boy brushed his hand over Pipicik's face.

(He does so, at the same time handing him a glittery headdress, which PIPICIK puts on.)

NARRATOR: Now Pipicik was all shiny and clean. Star Boy told him to tell their *koi'-yah* to prepare for his arrival. Now Pipicik went back home.

(PIPICIK gets into canoe and travels back to RAVEN'S house, while STAR BOY waits nearby.)

SCENE 6

(Setting: The same, a few minutes later.)

NARRATOR: When Pipicik arrived, Raven's curiosity was aroused.

(RAVEN enters.)

RAVEN: Look at Pipicik! He is different now! His face is sunshine!

(RAVEN exits.)

NARRATOR: Pipicik tells his *koi'-yah* about finding her lost son.

(ELDER SISTER enters.)

NARRATOR: He tells her that Star Boy wants to get married when he comes. She got busy right away and cleaned the house while Pipicik goes back to his brother.

(ELDER SISTER cleans the house – may use broom – while PIPICIK gets into the canoe and goes downstream to STAR BOY.)

NARRATOR: Star Boy is so powerful, he got a big elk.

(ELK enters. STAR BOY shoots it with his bow and arrows and it dies.)

NARRATOR: Pipicik helped his brother pack the elk into the canoe.

(They do so.)

NARRATOR: They planned that Star Boy would hide by lying down in the front of the canoe.

(STAR BOY lies in the canoe also and PIPICIK pulls wagon back to RAVEN'S house.)

NARRATOR: When they got home, a whole bunch of Indians went down to see them.

(RAVEN, MOLE, MAGPIE, MOUSE, FROG, GRANDMOTHER FROG, ELDERS, and other LUSHOOTSEED PEOPLE enter and watch PIPICIK'S arrival with awe.)

RAVEN: Look at Pipicik! He is different now! His face is sunshine!
NARRATOR: The people tried to see Star Boy but not one could because he was too bright.

(STAR BOY gets out of the canoe and ALL shield their eyes from his brightness.)

NARRATOR: Star Boy found his *koi'-yah* and hugged her and brushed his hands over her face. As he did so, she became bright and shiny too.

(He does so. As he brushes his hand over ELDER SISTER'S face, he hands her a glittery headdress, which she puts on.)

NARRATOR: Star Boy told his *koi'-yah* he wanted to get married.
STAR BOY: The one who can pack the meat from my canoe will be my wife!

MOUSE: I'm the one who can pack it!

(MOUSE tries to drag ELK out of the canoe while ALL heckle her or cheer her on. She cannot do it and gives up.)

MOLE: I'm the one who can pack it!

(MOLE tries to drag ELK out of the canoe while ALL heckle her or cheer her on. She cannot do it and gives up.)

MAGPIE: I'm the one who can pack it!

(MAGPIE tries to drag ELK out of the canoe while ALL heckle her or cheer her on. She cannot do it and gives up.)

NARRATOR: Nobody could lift it. Little Frog had a *kai'-yah,* a grandmother, who said:

GRANDMOTHER FROG: Frog, you might be the one packing that meat!

FROG: I'm too small to pack that heavy load!

GRANDMOTHER FROG: Go for the fun and try it.

FROG: *Aiii.*

(FROG tries to lift ELK out of the canoe while ALL heckle her or cheer her on. On her fourth try she succeeds and lays ELK on the ground.)

NARRATOR: She got a husband, that little thing! They butchered the elk.

(They haul ELK backstage and return with slabs of meat – may pantomime. ALL sit in or near RAVEN'S house and eat. FROG sits next to STAR BOY.)

NARRATOR: As soon as Raven is given the tallow he gulps it, gulps it, gulps it without chewing!

(He does so.)

NARRATOR: Raven is noted for his big appetite. Suddenly he said:

RAVEN: Uncover the roof! Uncover the roof! We are getting hot!

(They take off the roof of the house.)

NARRATOR: All of sudden RAVEN flew up to the roof!

(RAVEN "flies" up to the tabletop of his house, cawing.)

NARRATOR: He was flapping his wings and making such a racket! He was changed. He was changed by the one from the stars. He flew down river.

(He does so. The next two lines can be assigned to different characters if needed.)

ELDER #1: The high class one got changed!

ELDER #2: What will the coming people use for light?

NARRATOR: Now they would create the moon and the sun. Star Boy had the job of sunshine. All the Indians said:

ALL: *Aiii!!* Let's try it!

(STAR BOY goes up to the Sky and shines his light – use a small lamp. ALL react to it's brightness.)

ALL: It's too hot! It's too hot!

(ALL jump in the river to cool off.)

NARRATOR: Star Boy suggested that Pipicik be the sunshine. The Indians said:

ALL: *Aiii!!* Let's try it!

(PIPICIK goes up in the Sky and shines his light – use a smaller or less bright lamp that STAR BOY'S.)

ALL: It's just right!

NARRATOR: Star Boy was going to be the moon.

(STAR BOY & PIPICIK stand opposite each other in the Sky.)

NARRATOR: He came to count the months women have a baby in the belly. He put his wife right up on his chest.

(FROG goes up in the Sky and stands in front of STAR BOY.)

NARRATOR: That is why you can see a Frog on the moon! Now Star Boy and Pipicik decided to name the rivers and the lakes.

(STAR BOY & PIPICIK point to various places on earth, as they name rivers and lakes.)

STAR BOY: We'll name that one: Lake Washington *(Or substitute other local one.)*

PIPICIK: We'll name that one: The Columbia River *(Or substitute other local one.)*

(REPEAT the above, naming several rivers and lakes that are familiar to the actors.)

NARRATOR: When all the places had been named, the people sang their songs.

(ALL sing/dance "Where I Sit Is Holy" or other song.)

ALL: *Hoi'-yah!* The end!

(LIGHTS DOWN.)

APPENDIX A: VOCABULARY LIST
OF LUSHOOTSEED SALISH WORDS

LUSHOOTSEED	ENGLISH	PRONUNCIATION
aiii	yes	a'-eee
hoi'-yah	the end	hoy'-ah
huh-pai'	cedar	huh-pie'ee
kai'-yah	grandmother	ki'-yah
koi'-yah	mother	koy'-ah
tsi siab / siab	hello (said to females / males)	tsee' see-ab / see'-ab

APPENDIX B: SETS
SETS LIST:

SKY:
> 2 large, sturdy tables
> blue cloth, decorated as the sky and hung down the front of the tables
> strong tape
> paper ferns (taped near space between the 2 tables)
> backdrop (optional)

EARTH:
> long, blue cloth (river)
> campfire
> freestanding trees or bushes (optional)

RAVEN'S HOUSE:
> 1 sturdy table
> 2 freestanding, cardboard walls
> 1 large, cardboard piece (roof)

HOW TO MAKE THE SETS

FREESTANDING WALL (for Raven's house and trees & bushes)
- very large, cardboard box
- cardboard cutting knife
- scissors
- heavy butcher paper
- tape or glue
- markers, crayons or paint with brushes
- colored paper or fabric (optional)

Cut box to create a freestanding wall with accordion folds. Cut a piece of butcher paper to size of the wall. Tape or glue paper to the wall (if cardboard is plain white, you can eliminate this step). Draw picture of the set on the wall with markers, crayons, or paint. Colored paper or fabric can also be used to decorate the wall, using glue or tape. Silver tent can be covered with aluminum foil or silver paint, with top, the "roof," being covered with gold paper or paint.

LANDSCAPE BACKDROP
- heavy butcher paper
- sturdy tape
- markers, crayons or paint with brushes
- scissors

Cut butcher paper to fit across upstage wall. Draw sky pictures – stars, planets, clouds, and so on – with markers, crayons, or paint. Make sure the artists understand which end is up and that drawings must be large enough to be seen from the audience. Tape to wall.

CAMPFIRE
- several cardboard paper towel tubes or other cardboard pieces, rolled like logs
- flat piece of cardboard, approx. 30 cm. square
- red, orange and/or yellow tissue paper
- clear tape

Tape the tubes or other, log-shaped pieces of cardboard to the flat piece of cardboard. Tear the tissue paper into large pieces, stick them under and around the logs and tape with clear tape so that they jut up and out like flames.

APPENDIX C: PROPS

PROPS LIST

Bows & Arrows (for 2 Star Brothers and Star Boy)
2 Baskets
Ferns (paper)
Rope (pre-tied with slipknot)
Pillow (for Elder Sister – see Costumes)

Doll
Cradleboard
Diaper
Canoe
Paddle
Broom (optional)
Meat (optional)
2 Lamps (1 larger than the other)
3 Glittery Headdresses (see Costumes)

HOW TO MAKE THE PROPS

BOWS & ARROWS

- coat hangers
- string
- small pieces of cardboard
- scissors
- carrying bag for arrows
- heavy, brown paper bag or brown construction paper

- brown tape
- plastic straws
- colored construction paper
- clear tape

Unhook coat hanger, double over and bend into a half-moon shape. Wrap with a piece of brown paper and wrap with brown tape. Tie a length of string tautly between the two ends. Cut arrowhead out of cardboard, including a tab on the bottom. Insert the tab into the ends into the end of a straw and tape to secure. Cut feather out of construction paper, including a tab at the end. Insert the tab into the other end of the straw and tape to secure. Carrying bag for arrows should be slung over the shoulder or back. These bows and arrows are for show and don't really shoot well (fortunately).

CANOE

- child's wagon
- 2 large pieces of sturdy cardboard
- markers, crayons or paint with brushes
- butcher paper, scissors & glue (optional)

- cutting tool
- strong tape

Draw and cut cardboard in the shape of the sides of a canoe. Decorate with markers, crayons, or paint. (Cover first with butcher paper, if needed.) Secure cardboard to both sides of the wagon with tape. Actors can sit in the wagon and propel it with their feet while steering with the handle turned inward. When there are three actors in the canoe, one of them can simply walk in front and pull it (Raven pulls Elder Sister and Pipicik; Pipicik pulls Star Boy and Elk.)

PADDLE

- long pole or dowel

- pieces of thick cardboard
- cardboard cutting tool
- tape
- paint, as needed

Draw a circle on the cardboard, slightly oblong, and approx. 30 cm long. Draw a long tab at the bottom of it, for attaching the paddle to the pole. Cut out the paddle and place it near the top of the pole. Wrap tape around the tab, securing it to the pole. Paint as needed.

APPENDIX D: COSTUMES

COSTUME LIST

ELDER SISTER & YOUNGER SISTER: Indian costumes

WHITE STAR & BLUE STAR: all white and all blue costumes with stars and glitter and a glittery headdress

LOG PEOPLE & GRANDMOTHER LOG: brown pants & shirt or leotard & tights, with twigs and leaves (made of paper and taped on)

STAR BOY: bright, glittery costume with glittery headdress

DAYLIGHT GIRLS: fanciful costumes with stars and glitter and glittery headdresses

PIPICIK: Indian costume with glittery headdress

ELK: brown or black pants & shirt or leotard & tights, with horns and tail

RAVEN: black pants & shirt or leotard & tights, with feathered tail and headpiece

MOLE: brown or gray pants & shirt or leotard & tights, with dark glasses

MAGPIE: black pants & shirt or leotard & tights, with feathered tail and headpiece

MOUSE: mouse-colored pants & shirt or leotard & tights, with ears and tail

FROG & FROG GRANDMOTHER: green pants & shirt or leotard & tights

ELDERS & LUSHOOTSEED PEOPLE: Indian costumes

HOW TO MAKE THE COSTUMES:

GLITTERY HEADDRESSES
- glittery or colored pipe cleaners
- plastic headbands (optional)
- gold or silver paper or aluminum foil
- scissors
- clear tape

Either fashion headpieces out of pipe cleaners or use headbands. Cut stars out of paper or foil and either tape directly to the headpiece or to pipe cleaners which are then attached to headpiece by twisting the ends around it. Pipe cleaners can be shaped as rays or twisted into fanciful shapes.

ELK HORNS
- a small piece of brown, sturdy cardboard
- scissors
- wide, black elastic band, long enough to fit around actor's head
- stapler

Draw horns on the cardboard and cut out. Measure, cut, and staple the elastic to fit around the actor's head. Staple the horns to the elastic.

TAILS (Elk and Mouse)
- long strips, approx. 1 meter long, of colored chiffon or other light fabric
- scissors
- long, elastic strip or safety pins

Measure out three strips of fabric. Braid together and tie in a knot at either end. Tail is either pinned to back of actor's pants or tied to an elastic strip that is measured and tied to fit around actor's waist. The best place to pin the tail to pants is through belt loops. If you pin it directly to pants or shirt, it can rip the fabric if someone steps on the tail.

BIRD HEAD AND TAIL FEATHERS (Raven and Magpie)
- feathers (real or made out of paper)
- tape
- long, elastic strip
- string, scissors

Measure and tie the elastic to fit around the actor's head and waist. Cut string into several pieces, each approx. 30 cm long. Attach feathers all along the string pieces by wrapping a piece of tape around each feather stem and then wrapping it securely around the string. Tie the string pieces to the headband and waist band.

MOUSE EARS
- colored construction paper
- scissors
- light cardboard, glue (optional)
- markers, crayons, paint with brushes (optional)
- pencil
- stapler

Draw ears on paper and cut out. Cut a long strip of the same color paper, approximately 4 cm wide and long enough to go around the actor's head with a 2-3 cen-

timeters of overlap. Staple ears to strips, and staple strips to fit snugly around the actors' heads. You may want to reinforce ears and strips with a cardboard backing. Decorate as needed with markers, crayons, or paint.

APPENDIX E: SOUND & MUSIC

SOUND:
  Wind: a long, flexible plastic tube, whirled overhead
  Baby's Cry: voice from backstage
MUSIC:
  Song: "Pipicik's Crying Song" (included)
  Song: "Where I Sit Is Holy" (included)
  Other songs (optional)

APPENDIX F: LUSHOOTSEED SALISH CULTURE
Sources: Haboo, Native American Stories of Puget Sound by Vi Hilbert (University of Washington Press) and The Eye of the Changer by Muriel Ringstad (Alaska Northwest Publishing Company)

LITERATURE

In the past, all of the culture of the Lushootseed Salish people had to be committed to memory; thus, their historians developed excellent memories in order to pass on important information to later generations. When the culture was solely oral, as some elders would prefer to have it remain, the legends and other information were recited often in order to keep them alive and point out moral lessons. We do not know how long it has taken for these stories to come down to us, for they did not use the kind of calendar we use today. The Lushootseed peoples marked time by referring to remarkable occasions, such as the year of the solar eclipse or the time before the British people came. Today, the art of storytelling among the Lushootseed-speaking peoples is nearly forgotten as television and books have supplanted the roles of the Lushootseed raconteurs.

All of their legends are like gems with many facets. They need to be read, savored, and reread from many angles. Listeners are expected to listen carefully and learn why a story is being told. They are not told directly the meaning of the stories but are instead allowed the dignity of finding their own personal interpretation. All of the stories in Lushootseed culture are rich in humor, much of which pokes fun at pretentiousness. They can laugh at themselves and others in a way that is not malicious and which is mutually enjoyable and frequently uplifting.

LANGUAGE

Lushootseed is one of some twenty Native languages comprising the Salish family, spoken over much of Washington, British Columbia, and parts of Idaho, Montana, and Oregon. Lushootseed itself is the name of the Native language of the Puget Sound region, of which there are many dialects.

Translating the literature of one language into another is never easy, especially when the cultures involved are extremely dissimilar and when the translator must render in writing what has been an oral tradition. Subtleties of the Lushootseed language and oral delivery, such as tone of voice, vocal mannerisms, rhythm, pitch, and the effects of syntax and repetitions, cannot be fully expressed in written English. For example, there is no Lushootseed word for love, so it's meaning and nuances must be recognized from the signals expressed in the oral delivery.

In Lushootseed culture, everything is possible because they have no word for "can't." They also have no words that say "hello," "good morning," "good night," or "thank you." All these meanings are expressed through phrases or by physical gestures. For example, thankfulness is expressed by a phrase that translates as "You have done me a great favor/I appreciate what you have done for me" or by raising both arms and slightly moving the open palms up and down.

SPIRITUAL VALUES

All of the Lushootseed stories give expression to the most important values of the culture. These values, as remembered and translated by Vi Hilbert, are listed below. Many of the Lushootseed values are phrased in the negative but are here expressed in the positive:

Respect (Hold Sacred) all of the Earth
Respect (Hold Sacred) All of the Spirits
Remember (Hold Sacred) the Creator
Be Honest (Don't You Dare Lie!)
Be Generous (Be Helpful to Your People In Any Way You Can!)
Be Compassionate (Feel Forgiveness For Others!)
Be Clean (You Will Be Washed / Keep Washing Away All Badness [Dirt and Sin-Crime])
Be Industrious (And You Will Work Always, Don't Be Lazy!)

Today, many Lushootseed people are preserving and activating the spiritual beliefs of their ancestors. In the past, Lushootseed people believed they needed a spirit power to help them with special tasks. At around age four, boys went away by themselves to fast and wait for their spirit powers to make themselves known to them. Women also had spirit helpers for their special tasks.

Animals, fish, and everything in nature each possessed a spirit, just as humans do. Ceremonies were created to show good intentions to the spirits. For example, the bones of the salmon were thrown back in the water in order to thank the salmon spirits and so that new salmon would be generated from them.

SOCIAL VALUES

Lushootseed peoples are told again and again not to disgrace themselves or their people under any circumstances. Still, they appreciate anyone smart enough to get something done by fooling someone else. Their stories are often about people with animal names so that the humor of human foibles and frailties can be more openly laughed about.

In public, however, Native people take care not to make anyone feel embarrassed or unwanted, and they genuinely appreciate differences between people. Although the characters in their stories often get themselves in lots of trouble, they are not wiped out at the end. Instead, they are allowed to stew in their own folly, and figure their own way out of the situation. Disapproval of bad habits or behavior is shown by temporarily ignoring someone or by ridiculing them, but this is meant as a way to help the person overcome their problem. It is believed that ultimately, everyone should be made to feel welcome and important.

HOUSING

In the past, the Lushootseed lived in villages of four or five cedar plank houses, called longhouses. Each longhouse sheltered several related families and as many as forty people lived in each one. The longhouses measured approximately one hundred feet long and forty feet wide. They were dark and smoky inside, as the doorway was small and there were no windows. A plank in the roof was lifted up to let out smoke from the cooking fires. Fires were kept burning on the dirt floor in front of each family's quarters. From the ceiling hung chunks of smoked salmon, strings of smoked clams, and dried root and herbs.

Along the inside walls were built two wide platforms, one above the other. The people slept on the upper platform and worked on the lower one, which was wider. The space underneath the lower platform was used for storage. The women sewed cattail leaves together for mats, which were hung between each family's section for privacy and warmth. Mattresses and sitting pads were also made of woven cattails.

CLOTHING

Their clothing was made of cedar bark which had been shredded and pounded. Robes and blankets were made of shredded cedar bark mixed with fireweed fluff and feathers or dog or goat wool, or were made of bird or animal skins or furs sewn together. Ponchos were made of cattail leaves and hats were made of tightly twined cedar bark.

UTENSILS & TOOLS

Kitchen utensils were carved out of wood by the men. The women made mats and baskets of grasses, roots, twigs, and other materials gathered during the summer. These materials were soaked and split, cured, and sometimes dyed. They had no metal. Tools were made of horn, bone, or stone, with wooden handles. To cook, women heated stones in a fire and then, using greenwood tongs, placed the stones into tightly coiled cedar root baskets. When the stones cooled, they were replaced with hot ones from the fire.

CANOES

Their way of life was based on canoes. Canoes were made of dugout cedar logs and their size and shape depended on their use. Sharp-ended canoes with high prows were for rough water, as the prows could cut through the water like a wedge and blunt-ended canoes were for use on rivers and still waters. The canoes were thirty to fifty feet long and could carry twenty to thirty people and their luggage. Extra curved projections at the bow and stern were carved from separate pieces of cedar and attached to the canoes with pegs and withes of thin cedar limbs. Canoes in use were kept floating in the cove in front of the village. Those not in use were turned over on the beach above the tide line and covered with mats to protect them from the sun.

WHERE I SIT IS HOLY

Moderato

Where I sit is ho - ly, ho - ly is the ground. For - est, moun- tain, ri - ver, lis - ten to the sound: Great Spi - rit cir - cling all a - round me.

PIPICIK'S CRYING SONG

tune: Pamela Gerke

Oh woe, oh woe, oh woe It is said my bro-ther was sto - len by wo - men who be -longed up riv - er. I'm from the wring- ing of my koi - yah I've been made a slave by Rav - en.

BIBLIOGRAPHY

Arkhurst, Joyce Cooper. *The Adventures of Spider.* Boston: Little, Brown & Co., 1964.

Haviland, Virginia. *Favorite Fairy Tales Told in Ireland.* Boston: Little, Brown & Co., 1966.

Hilbert, Vi. *Haboo: Lushootseed Literature in English* (originally titled *Huboo*) Seattle: Vi Hilbert, 1980.

Jablow, Alta and Withers, Carl. *The Man In The Moon: Sky Tales From Many Lands.* New York: Holt, Rinehart & Winston, 1969. As retold from Mostaert, Anoine, *Folklore Ordos.* Peiping: Monumenta Serica, No. 11, Catholic University.

Kimishima, Hisako. *Ma Lien and the Magic Paintbrush.* New York: Parent's Magazine Press, 1968. Originally published by Kaisei Sha, Tokyo.

Marxer, Marcy. *Jump Children.* (Tape/CD includes song: "January, February, March") Rounder Records, 1-800-44-DISCS.

Ransome, Arthur. *Old Peter's Russian Tales.* London: Thomas Nelson & Sons, Ltd., 1971.

Wiggin, Kate Douglas and Smith, Nora Archibald. *The Fairy Ring.* Garden City: Doubleday, 1956.

PAMELA GERKE has been Director and Playwright for Kids Action Theater Play Productions in Seattle since she founded it in 1988. She has written and produced over twenty-five children's plays, as well as being composer and music director for several other shows. Pamela has worked as a children's music and movement specialist for over ten years and currently divides her time between Kids Action Theater, conducting the Seattle Women's Ensemble (adult chorus) and a children's choir, private piano instruction, and composing and arranging music for choruses and for theater.